The Erotics of Domination

OKLAHOMA SERIES IN CLASSICAL CULTURE

Oklahoma Series in Classical Culture

SERIES EDITOR

Ellen Greene, *University of Oklahoma*

ADVISORY BOARD

Susan Guettel Cole, *State University of New York, Buffalo*
Carolyn J. Dewald, *Bard College*
Thomas M. Falkner, *The College of Wooster*
Elaine Fantham, *Princeton University*
Nancy Felson, *University of Georgia*
Helene P. Foley, *Barnard College*
Sara Mack, *University of North Carolina, Chapel Hill*
Thomas R. Martin, *College of the Holy Cross*
John F. Miller, *University of Virginia*
Jon Solomon, *University of Arizona*
Richard F. Thomas, *Harvard University*

THE EROTICS OF DOMINATION

Male Desire

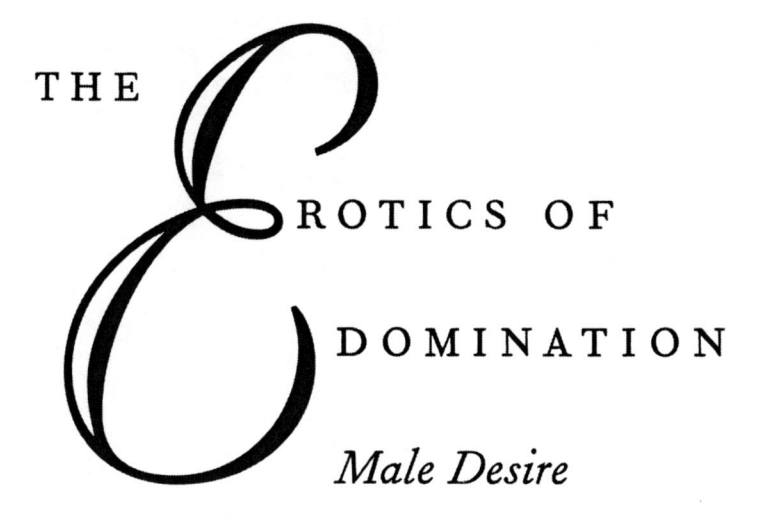

and the Mistress

in Latin Love Poetry

Ellen Greene

UNIVERSITY OF OKLAHOMA PRESS
NORMAN

Library of Congress Cataloging-in-Publication Data

Greene, Ellen, 1950–
    The erotics of domination : male desire and the mistress in Latin love poetry / Ellen Greene.
    p.   cm.
    Includes bibliographical references (p.   ) and index.
    ISBN 978-0-8061-4050-6 (paper)
    1. Love poetry, Latin—History and criticism.   2. Ovid, 43 B.C.–17 or 18 A.D.—Criticism and interpretation.   3. Catullus, Gaius Valerius—Criticism and interpretation.   4. Propertius, Sextus—Criticism and interpretation.   5. Erotic poetry, Latin—History and criticism.   6. Man-woman relationships in literature.   7. Dominance (Psychology) in literature.   8. Masculinity in literature.   9. Violence in literature.   10. Desire in literature.   11. Rome—In literature.   12. Sex in literature.   I. Title.
PA6029.L6G74   1998
871'.01093543—dc21   98-7942
                                                                                                            CIP

Erotics of Domination: Male Desire and the Mistress in Latin Love Poetry is Volume 37 in the Oklahoma Series in Classical Culture.

The Erotics of Domination: Male Desire and the Mistress in Latin Love Poetry, by Ellen Greene, was originally published in hard cover by The Johns Hopkins University Press, 2715 N. Charles Street, Baltimore, MD 21218. Copyright © 1998 by The Johns Hopkins University Press. Copyright transferred to the author 2008. Oklahoma paperback edition published by the University of Oklahoma Press, Publishing Division of the University, 2010, by arrangement with The Johns Hopkins Press.

All rights reserved. No part of this publication may be reproduced, stored in a retrieval system, or transmitted, in any form or by any means, electronic, mechanical, photocopying, recording, or otherwise—except as permitted under Section 107 or 108 of the United States Copyright Act—without the prior written permission of the University of Oklahoma Press.

To Jim

Contents

Acknowledgments   *ix*

Introduction   *xi*

CHAPTER 1. The Catullan *Ego:*
Fragmentation and the Erotic Self   *1*

CHAPTER 2. Gendered Domains:
Public and Private in Catullus   *18*

CHAPTER 3. Elegiac Woman: Fantasy, *Materia,*
and Male Desire in Propertius' *Monobiblos*   *37*

CHAPTER 4. Ovid's *Amores:*
Women, Violence, and Voyeurism   *67*

CHAPTER 5. Sexual Politics in Ovid's
Amores   *93*

Notes   *115*

Bibliography   *129*

Index   *137*

Acknowledgments

The University of Oklahoma provided generous financial support that allowed me to complete this book. A research grant from the Oklahoma Foundation for the Humanities contributed to freeing up my time as well. I am especially grateful to my colleagues in the classics department at the University of Oklahoma, particularly my department chair Jack Catlin, for providing me with a stimulating and supportive environment in which to think and write.

I owe special thanks to William S. Anderson, whose insight and steady encouragement guided and sustained me at earlier stages of this project. I am indebted as well to friends, colleagues, and mentors who offered help and encouragement on parts of this work while it was in progress, including Ronnie Ancona, Harriette Andreadis, Karen Bassi, Mary-Kay Gamel, Tom Habinek, David Larmour, Allen Miller, and Thomas Rosenmeyer. I also wish to express my gratitude to Elizabeth Asmis, George Kennedy, Eleanor Winsor Leach, and several anonymous referees for their useful criticism and much-needed encouragement on parts of this book which appeared as articles in *Classical Philology* and *American Journal of Philology*.

I am very grateful to Doug Armato, editor at The Johns Hopkins University Press, for his enthusiastic support of this project and for his perceptive editorial eye, which helped to make this a better book.

In addition, I am deeply appreciative of the love and moral support of my family, Sid and Florence Schiffman, and my sister, Debra Schiffman.

Last, and most of all, I thank Jim for everything.

Introduction

This book examines portrayals of women and conceptions of gender in the love poetry of Catullus, Propertius, and Ovid. I investigate aspects of Roman elegy which point to some of the ways Latin love poets perpetuate traditional conceptions of women, of female sexuality, and of the woman's role in amatory relationships. Although the study of "women in antiquity" has, over the past twenty years, become a well-established area of inquiry within classical studies,[1] for the most part, feminist research in classics has directed its attention to the study of "woman" herself, either as the subject of retrievable historical data or as an object of representation. Recent work in the study of gender as a category of investigation, however, has altered the way feminist critics approach the analysis of literary texts. Feminist criticism, including the study of "women in antiquity," particularly in the 1970s and early 1980s, focused on a kind of compensatory scholarship by emphasizing women's history, gynocriticism, and psychology. Yet as the theorist Jane Flax points out, such woman-centered investigation "ironically privileges the man as unproblematic or exempted from determination by gender relations."[2] Thus, the problematization of gender relations, Flax argues, "is the single most important advance in feminist theory."[3]

With the rise of gender theory and criticism, feminist critics attend not only to "woman" as a subject of investigation but also to men as integral to an understanding of the social processes that determine and constitute relations between the sexes. Feminist criticism, then, interrogates "masculinity" as part of a complex set of social relations in which men and women are both seen as governed by cultural stereotypes and ideologies. A crucial aspect of the problematization of gender relations in feminist theory is the notion that gender is not merely a question of sexual difference but also of power, inequality, and male domination over women.[4] Accordingly, if we regard men's writing as a gendered discourse, then we must address the whole spectrum of gender assumptions in male-authored texts.

Consequently, in my discussion of Roman amatory texts my aim is to offer explanations of Roman assumptions and ideologies of gender which involve eliciting the symbolic meanings ascribed in literary discourse to sex-based gender identities. Although there have been several important studies of the role of women in Latin love poetry,[5] there have not been any book-length studies of how gender and gender roles are constructed in those texts. My study focuses on the ways gender ideology is inscribed, represented, and reproduced in the literary discourses of Roman amatory texts. Further, I hope to show that much of the criticism of the Latin love poets has also been inscribed with "male" readings, that is, critical approaches that are limited by an identification with the perspectives and values of the male narrator. As Ronnie Ancona points out in her discussion of Horace's love poetry, the reliance on the poet as guide to his own love poems often leads to a critical approach that "remains trapped in male assumptions about desire," assumptions that cannot be questioned. The issues Ancona raises are that traditional criticism of Latin love poetry has tended to privilege and romanticize the male perspective of the poetic narrator and that the gender specificity of desire in Roman amatory texts has often been ignored.[6]

The discourses of male desire in Latin love poetry, I will argue, demonstrate that love (*amor*) is intimately bound up with the hierarchies and social inequalities in the power systems of Roman politics. Amatory discourse in Roman love poetry cannot, I believe, be dissociated from male assumptions about desire which reflect the hegemonic discourses of a patriarchal value system. As Michel Foucault has shown in *The History of Sexuality*, Greco-Roman erotic relations pivoted on patterns of dominance and submission, patterns that both affirmed and consolidated social and political hierarchies. In the Greco-Roman model, true masculinity was attained only after an adolescent boy passed through the stage of passivity and feminization (i.e., objectification). His masculinity in adulthood depended on control over his *domus* (household), over political and economic affairs, and, most importantly, over himself. Maintaining that control so important to Roman "masculinity" meant constant attention to any deterioration in social status, to the mastery over one's appetites, and to moral fortitude. Indeed, any loss of vitality resulting from sickness, old age, or overindulgence in physical pleasure, any lapse of moral resolve were threats to the preservation of masculine identity. Ancient masculinity is thus always at risk, but never so much as in the presence of the sexually wanton female, whose erotic impulses are imagined to be inexhaustible. The instability of Roman "masculinity" is perhaps nowhere more evident than in the amatory texts of Roman poets. Catullus' Lesbia poems show a constant tension between the male lover's assertion of his moral resolve and his reversion to a "womanish" state in which he lapses into powerlessness and emotionality. The diminution of the Catullan lover's "maleness" when confronted by a woman he regards and depicts as sexually wanton, as we will see, allows Catullus to reveal the fragmenting effects of *amor* on the self.

Whereas the Catullan lover appears to struggle against his own "feminization," the Roman elegiac poets—particularly Propertius and Ovid—proclaim in their poems a radically unconventional philosophy of life through their apparently deliberate inversion of conventional sex roles—in which women are portrayed as dominant and men as subservient. Roman elegiac poetry is predicated entirely on clearly defined roles for the speaker and his mistress. The conventional stance of the elegiac lover is one of enslavement to his emotions and of servitude to his mistress. That servitude, at least nominally, accords the lover's mistress complete domination and control over him. Catullus and Propertius, for example, often refer to their mistresses as *dominae* or slave-mistresses who subject their lovers to the torments of abandonment and betrayal. The elegist, typically, portrays the male in the traditional female role of devoted, dependent, and passive and at the same time gives masterful, active conduct to his mistress.

Another way in which the elegist identifies himself with the traditional female role is by explicitly advocating a life of leisure, love, and pleasure to the exclusion of conventional masculine pursuits—law, politics, and the military. The elegist, in fact, codifies these unorthodox attitudes into a flagrantly provocative, alternative social creed. Although the elegists renounce conventional masculine attitudes and values, they nonetheless use political and military terminology to describe the lover's relationship with his mistress. This adoption of political vocabulary in the private sphere of love has been generally understood by scholars to mean that elegists elevate in importance traditional female concerns (the life of love) to a status that equals accepted male pursuits. I will argue, however, that the use of military and political language to describe amatory relations suggests, instead, a redefinition of the erotic life in terms of the traditionally male ethic of domination and competition.

In addition, I will show how a progressive objectification and dehumanization of the female occur in elegy through the poet's identification of the elegiac woman as *materia* (subject, matter) for his writing. My study will attempt to demonstrate that the apparent elevated stature of women in Latin love poetry does not portray them as subjects in their own right but rather as objects of male fantasies of erotic domination. I shall argue that the subordination of the woman as beloved to the woman as *materia* reveals a version of male desire which devalues women and turns them into commodities of exchange in two senses: between their husbands and lovers and between the poet and the literary marketplace.

My first chapter, "The Catullan *Ego:* Fragmentation and the Erotic Self," examines the divided consciousness of the Catullan "I" through an analysis of the dynamic, shifting relationships of multiple speaking voices in several of Catullus' poems about his mistress Lesbia. I show that the multivoiced *ego* in Catullus' poems does not merely dramatize ambivalence but illustrates in a more general way the fragmenting effects of amatory experience and the paradoxes inherent in amatory discourse. As one important aspect of this fragmentation, I discuss the vacillation between "masculine" and "feminine" voices attached to the voice of the speaker and the voice identified as "Catullus." I explore the tension in Catullus' poems between the voice of "feminine" helplessness and hysteria (expressed as the voice of the abandoned woman) and a "masculine" voice that the feminized male lover calls up in himself to rescue him from the destructive effects of *amor*.

In the second chapter, "Gendered Domains: Public and Private in Catullus," I discuss three poems that epitomize Catullus' attitudes toward the public domain: 5, 7, and 11. In these three poems, Catullus expresses what seem to be conflicting positions about traditional male cultural discourses and practices. I interrogate those conflicting attitudes in light of Catullus' inversion of gender roles to elucidate the ways gender ideology is inscribed in poems that explicitly address or use the public domain as a focal point of self-definition for the speaker. I also explore the paradoxical figure of Lesbia as a vehicle, on the one hand, for the speaker's antimasculine ideal and, on the other hand, for his stereotypical misogynistic attitudes.

My third chapter, "Elegiac Woman: Fantasy, *Materia*, and Male Desire in Propertius' *Monobiblos*," analyzes Propertius' portrayal of his mistress Cynthia in 1.1, 1.3, and 1.11. I argue that Propertius presents his elegiac mistress as a pictorial object that arouses the lover's erotic fantasies *and* serves as a vehicle for his literary fame. Despite Propertius' representation of Cynthia as both *dura* (strong) and *docta* (learned), the male narrator in 1.3 and 1.11 imagines his mistress either in an ideal state of captivity and helplessness (1.3), or he identifies her exclusively with nonrational nature — with the disruptive and dangerous sensuality that poses a threat to the perpetuation of Roman cultural values (1.11). In both cases, I argue that Propertius entraps Cynthia within a discursive practice that preserves her object status and places her in a symbolic order structured around male fantasies of control over women's sexuality and autonomy.

The fourth chapter of this book, "Ovid's *Amores:* Women, Violence, and Voyeurism," argues that, unlike Propertius, who never abandons the elegiac fiction of sexual role inversion, Ovid shatters the fiction of the male narrator as enslaved and the female narrative subject as his enslaver. Ovid accomplishes this by implicating his narrator in a multitude of contradictions and letting the reader "see through" his manipulations and exploitations of women. Thus, I explore how Ovid's poems reveal the mechanics of male discourses of power and domination over women. My analysis focuses on the visual figuration of "masculine" and "feminine" positions in *Amores* 1.3, 1.5, and 1.7. I show how the elegiac mistress becomes the object of the narrator's voyeuristic gaze and how the configuration of seer and seen revolves on a pattern of male dominance and female submission—despite the apparent reversal of traditional gender roles in elegiac poetry. My discussion of the three poems demonstrates that the objectification of the woman fixed in the position of icon, spectacle, or image to be looked at is linked to the sexual pleasure of the narrator enacted through his violent domination and devaluation of his mistress.

The fifth and final chapter of the book, "Sexual Politics in Ovid's *Amores,*" shows how Ovid goes much further than Propertius in suggesting that the identification of the elegiac mistress as *materia* implies an inherent dehumanization and exploitation of women. The later poems in the *Amores*, particularly those in the third book, give a more blatant picture of the male lover's deception and exploitation of women than we see in the earlier books. By portraying the elegiac lover flagrantly using his mistress as his poetic *materia* for the sake of his personal and professional profit, Ovid deconstructs the romantic rhetoric of his poetic predecessors and reveals what he believes to be the hypocrisy in the elegiac pose. The narrator's conspicuous indifference to the moral implications of his amatory practices conveys Ovid's attempt to destroy the myth of the elegiac lover as the upholder of an ideal that is morally superior to the conventional values of Roman society. Ovid presents a view of Roman society which sanctions brutality toward women—particularly in poems that show open adultery in which women are treated as commodities of exchange between their husbands and their lovers. Moreover, I argue that through the way in which his male lover links sexual "pandering" with Rome's hegemony, Ovid suggests a close alliance between male sexual dominance and the assertion of political control and aggression.

Roman poets before Ovid, to be sure, criticize values of commercialism in Roman society; but, as I argue in the final chapter, Ovid's poetic predecessors portrayed the erotic and imaginative life as offering, at least potentially, a refuge from the degradation in the exterior world. Ovid, on the other hand, demonstrates that rather than provide a moral alternative, *amor* often reiterates the mercantilist and imperialist values in Augustan culture. Ovid's demystification of the elegiac poet's avowed commitment to moral ideals questions and destabilizes ideologies of erotic conquest and domination. More than that, Ovid's poems show us the potential moral excesses in the assertion of masculine privilege and authority. By stripping away any illusions or ideals from the lover's amatory practices and showing how the lover is oblivious to the moral implications of his duplicity and need to conquer, Ovid exposes the competitive and violent attitudes that can pervade *amor*—attitudes with broad cultural implications that embrace *both* genders.

The Erotics of Domination

CHAPTER ONE

The Catullan *Ego*
Fragmentation and the Erotic Self

PERHAPS THE MOST STRIKING and consistent feature of Catullus' Lesbia poems is his vivid expression of erotic ambivalence.[1] The Catullan lover reveals his burning passion for his mistress and, at the same time, his rational awareness that his desires conflict with his erotic ideals. The logical analysis that the Catullan lover brings to bear on his irrational emotions often creates a fragile tension between logical structure and emotional rhetoric, a tension that allows Catullus to exploit the gap between reason and passion.[2] A number of scholars have focused on the conflicting kinds of love expressed in the Lesbia poems and on the complementary relations of logic and emotion.[3] I believe further light can be shed on the divided consciousness of the Catullan *ego* through an analysis of the dynamic, shifting relationships of multiple speaking voices in Catullus' anguished poems about Lesbia. I will argue that the multivoiced *ego* in Catullus' poems does not merely dramatize ambivalence in the lover's feelings toward his mistress but illustrates in a more general way the fragmenting effects of *amor* on the self.[4] In her book *Catullan Self-Revelation*, Eve Adler interprets the shifting of persons in Catullus' poems as an expression of "anguished self-division." But her conclusion that the "speaking I" is the voice of Catullus himself, "a particular and knowable person who in fact wants to be known by us," offers an unsatisfying account of Catullus' literary strategies. We cannot assume that the *ego* presented to us in Catullus' poems represents "the unique lived experience of the person" (7).

Indeed, the complex configuration of voices and speakers in many of the Lesbia poems suggests rather a confusion of identity which makes it impossible to associate Catullus' poetic ego with any particular person outside the poem. I shall refer to Catullus only when I am speaking about the poet as the creator and manipulator of the various voices within the poems. When I discuss "Catullus" I will be referring to the figure of "Catullus" as an object of address for the speaking "I." Catullus' poems, indeed, defy the conventional opposition of poet and persona. The traditional concept of a persona—an autonomous unified consciousness within the text—cannot capture the indeterminate fragmentary quality of the Catullan "I." I agree with Micaela Janan's formulation of the "I" in Catullus' poems as "the grammatical subject, governed from outside itself by rules of grammar and syntax making up a linguistic structure.... The subject is thus the vector product of all the forces in play at the site of consciousness at any time."[5] I hope to show that Catullus' speaking "I" is not a determinate entity at all but rather a polysemous subject that cannot be reduced to a unified meaning or a single set of practices and discourses. I shall argue that, rather than revealing the truth of who Catullus is, Catullus' use of multiple speaking voices[6] dramatizes the fragmenting effects of amatory experience and reveals paradoxes that inhere in erotic discourse. As Roland Barthes observes in *A Lover's Discourse*, the lover's impulse to understand his madness results in a divided self: "To understand—is that not to divide the image, to undo the *I*, proud organ of misapprehension?" (60).

I will examine Poems 8, 72, and 76 to illustrate how Catullus employs multiple speaking voices to dramatize the lover's divided consciousness. These three poems are among the most compelling examples of this phenomenon in the Catullan *corpus*.[7]

Poem 8

Poem 8 is a good place to begin our discussion because the issues of identity and allocution are especially problematic in light of the configuration of three persons in the poem: the speaker, the second-person addressee identified as "Catullus," and another "Catullus" referred to in the third person.[8]

> Miser Catulle, desinas ineptire,
> et quod vides perisse perditum ducas.
> fulsere quondam candidi tibi soles,

The Catullan *Ego*

```
         cum ventitibas quo puella ducebat
 5       amata nobis quantum amabitur nulla.
         ibi illa multa tum iocosa fiebant,
         quae tu volebas nec puella nolebat.
         fulsere vere candidi tibi soles.
         nunc iam illa non vult: tu quoque.
10       impote(ns noli),
         nec quae fugit sectare, nec miser vive,
         sed obstinata mente perfer, obdura.
         vale. puella. iam Catullus obdurat,
         nec te requiret nec rogabit invitam:
15       at tu dolebis, cum rogaberis nulla.
         scelesta, vae te. quae tibi manet vita?
         quis nunc te adibit? cui videberis bella?
         quem nunc amabis? cuius esse diceris?
         quem basiabis? cui labella mordebis?
20       at tu, Catulle, destinatus obdura.
```

[Poor Catullus, stop your folly, and account as lost what you see is lost. Once the days shone bright on you, when you used to go where she led, she who was loved by me as no one will ever be loved. There so many joys were ours, which you desired nor did she turn away. Bright to you, truly, shone the days. Now she desires no more—no more should you desire, madman, nor follow her who flees, nor live in misery, but endure with a resolute mind, be firm. Farewell, my dear. Now Catullus is firm; he will not seek you nor ask you against your will. But you will be sorry, when no one wants you. Poor wretch, what life remains for you? Who now will come to you? Who will think you beautiful? Whom now will you love? By whose name will you be called? Whom will you kiss? Whose lips will you bite? But you, Catullus, be resolved and firm.]

The dramatic structure of the poem as well as the self-presentation of the speaker depend on the discontinuity of past and present, then and now. The speaker is both lamenting and renouncing an ideal past in which the speaker's love for his mistress was fulfilled. Throughout the poem the speaker vacillates between conjuring up his lost happiness and attempting to renounce his passion and finally accept Lesbia's rejection of him. The poem is built on a hard structure of imperatives in which the speaker tries to reprove himself for clinging to the past and for being incapable of giving up his love, despite the girl's rejection of him. As Eduard Fraenkel observes, the imperative tone in the poem is reinforced by Catullus' uncharacteristic deviation from his usual practice of enjambment.[9] This lack of enjambment produces a hard rhythm and keeps to the tone of the speaker trying to whip himself into shape.

The vacillations of the poem between past and present, between resolution and romantic nostalgia, correspond to the way the speaker vacillates between referring to himself in the second and third persons. In the first line the speaker begins by addressing "Catullus" directly in the second person and immediately attributes foolishness (*ineptire*) to his persistent love for his mistress. From this first line, the disparity between the perspectives of the speaker and "*Miser Catulle*" is made clear. Catullus' strategy here in separating the speaker from the wretched fool who clings helplessly to an ideal past brings home the fact that the speaker is hopelessly divided between his ability to see his foolishness so clearly and his inability to stop himself from continuing to be drawn back into the past and into the constellation of emotions associated with that past. The second line of the poem reinforces the sense of disparity in the split between speaker and obsessive lover by juxtaposing *vides* and *ducas*. For "Catullus" to accept his position would mean that he would have to be able to deduce (*ducas*) rationally an appropriate mode of behavior and feeling from actual experience (*vides*).

The speaker's difficulty in persuading "Catullus" to take this rational approach is evidenced in lines 3–8. The quick shift from *ducas*, with its sense of hard reality, to *fulsere* in the next line, which immediately transports us to the shimmering images of the past, bears witness to how compelling that past still is for the speaker. Although the speaker is clearly trying to dissuade "Catullus" from his silly passion with the *puella*, his nostalgic imaginings of past erotic fulfillment confuse the distinction between the speaker and "Catullus" the tormented lover. This dramatizes the difficulty of Catullus overcoming his passion by showing how difficult it is to stand back coolly and comment on his desires. Moreover, the speaker's sudden shift from addressing "Catullus" as *you* to referring to himself in the first person in line 5 (*amata nobis*), in the context of "Catullus' " erotic past, serves to confound the detached persona of the speaker and the frenzied, lovesick "Catullus." As in the previous lines, the sharp juxtaposition of line 8 (*fulsere vere candidi tibi soles*), which is the culmination of the images of an ideal past, with the jarring *nunc* in the next line plunges the speaker back into the harsh present reality of Lesbia's rejection of "Catullus." As past and present, speaker and addressee merge in the evocation of erotic union, the sense of a poetic voice that incorporates the positions of both the lover's folly and the speaker's rational wisdom gains in clarity, so that what we end up with is a narrator whose identity is defined by the very oppositions that divide him. The attempt to bring back the image of the beloved and the past romantic happiness he shared with her has the effect of momentarily creating a new sense of time so that the past irradiates the present moment of discourse and generates a present reality that is suffused with the light of memory and imagination.

We can see to what extent the speaker's memory has taken hold by noticing the way *fulsere quondam candidi tibi soles* (line 3) changes to *fulsere vere candidi tibi soles* in line 8. The transformation from *quondam* to *vere* signals the change in the speaker's mind from distanced reflection on the past to a complete absorption in it. For a moment the past becomes present reality at the same time as the voices of speaker and lover are confounded. The voice that we now hear is a voice that is fragmented, divided between past and present, cool reflection and intense emotional involvement. Even though the moment of imaginative re-creation of erotic union is a discrete unit in the poem, bound by the repetition of lines beginning and ending with *fulsere* and *soles*, the black cloud of loss and separation in an *actual* present hovers over the *candidi soles* of the past. Roland Barthes captures the paradox of the speaker-lover caught between then and now, between the powerlessness of his emotional responses and the power of his discourse.

> Endlessly I sustain the discourse of the beloved's absence; actually a preposterous situation; the other is absent as referent, present as allocutory. This singular distortion generates a kind of insupportable present; I am wedged between two tenses, that of the reference and that of the allocution: you have gone (which I lament), you are here (since I am addressing you). Whereupon I know what the present, that difficult tense, is: a pure portion of anxiety. Absence persists — I must endure it. Hence I will *manipulate* it: transform the distortion of time into oscillation, produce rhythm, make an entrance onto the stage of language.[10]

At line 9, however, speaker and lover separate into distinct voices once again at the moment when the speaker's awareness of "Catullus'" situation returns. Paradoxically, the "entrance onto the stage of language" has only made clear the extent to which the speaker is incapable of curing "Catullus" of his attachment to the *puella*. When the speaker breaks away from his imaginative vision of past happiness and calls "Catullus" "*impotens*," it is also an expression of his own "impotence" in being unable to persuade "Catullus" to stop desiring the *puella*. We can hear desperation and urgency in the word *impotens* in that it again links speaker and lover in their mutual failure. This urgency is reinforced in the repetition of negatives in the speaker's exhortations to "Catullus" to stop pursuing (*sectare*) the *puella* and to stop wallowing in his misery (*nec miser vive*).

In her discussion of Poem 8, Eve Adler makes the point that at the heart of the speaker's strategy in trying to cure "Catullus" of his lovesickness is his attempt to subvert the experience "Catullus" had by exposing "Catullus'" utter passivity in his love affair with his mistress.[11] The girl led, "Catullus" followed, and joys *happened* to him. Once the *puella* stops loving, then "Catullus'" desire seems all the more pathetic, and his status of being *impotens* is thrown into sharp relief. The logic of such a strategy would be to trick "Catullus" into decisive action by making his behavior seem not only silly but morally weak and undignified.

Another current in this argument, which Adler does not take up, is the vacillation between masculine and feminine voices that are attached, respectively, to the voices of the speaker and "Catullus." As we move back and forth between the perspective of the speaker urging "Catullus" to be reasonable and resist his passions like a man and the perspective of the lover who is as weak willed and indecisive as a woman, we can see that the voice of the abandoned woman figures prominently in Catullus' poems.[12] The speaker's identification of "Catullus" as *impotens* reinforces an association between the lover "Catullus" and feminine powerlessness and emotionality.

In his book *Abandoned Women and Poetic Tradition*, Lawrence Lipking observes that "when a man is abandoned, in fact, he feels like a woman" (xix). Lipking goes further in saying that in the history of poetry, men come to learn about themselves (a world of feelings opens up to them) through the experience of abandonment and loss. But, as Lipking argues, the pathos of the abandoned man's situation depends on the assumption that men are *supposed* to be masters. We can see in Poem 8 that the speaker by no means gives himself over to his feelings of abandonment. The abandoned man regards his abandonment as unnatural, or at least partialized, and he therefore must counterbalance it with "manly" resentment. It is perfectly natural then for Catullus to have the voice of the speaker in his poem as an antipode to the feminized voice of the pathetic, abandoned lover.

I turn to Barthes for his insight into the phenomenon of the abandoned man:

> Historically, the discourse of absence is carried on by the Woman: Woman is sedentary, Man hunts, journeys; Woman is faithful (she waits), man is fickle (he sails away, he cruises). It is Woman who gives shape to absence, elaborates its fiction, for she has time to do so; she weaves and she sings; the

> Spinning Songs express both immobility (by the hum of the Wheel) and absence (far away, rhythms of travel, sea surges, cavalcades). It follows that in any man who utters the other's absence *something feminine* is declared: this man who waits and who suffers from his waiting is miraculously feminized.[13]

The conflict in the poem between the voices of feminine emotionality and manly self-control must be understood in the context of Roman moralizing discourse, with its anxieties about gender, social status, and political power. As Catharine Edwards demonstrates, morality and masculinity are inextricable from one another as distinguishing features of "Romanness."[14] Virtue, Edwards argues, is coextensive with masculinity and necessarily involves a high degree of self-control, particularly with respect to indulgence in pleasure. Thus a lack of control over one's emotions or desires would be considered "unmanly." When the speaker in Poem 8 tells "Catullus" to "endure" and "be hard," he is speaking in the language of conventional Roman morality and associating "Catullus'" "feminine" behavior with moral weakness. In the process of trying to "overcome" his unruly emotions, the feminized male lover calls up in himself the masculine voice that he hopes will rescue him.

We hear that masculine voice trying desperately to counterbalance the images of lost happiness by exhorting "Catullus" to stop feeling like a woman and start thinking and acting like a man (*sed obstinata mente perfer, obdura*, line 12). In the next line, however, when the speaker suddenly apostrophizes the *puella*, we are no longer sure whether the voice is that of the speaker or the lover "Catullus." Throughout the poem the *puella* is associated with "Catullus" and his particular erotic experience, and the speaker stands apart, admonishing and advising "Catullus," consistently referring to the *puella* in the third person. But suddenly, in line 13, the speaker addresses his mistress directly with the implicit claim that the speaker has been successful in dissuading "Catullus" from his silly passion. For a moment it seems as though the voices of speaker and lover have merged. But immediately after addressing the *puella* directly, the speaker refers to "Catullus" in the third person, which suggests that speaker and lover continue to be split from one another and that the speaker has not yet resolved his conflict between his rationality and his unreasonable desires for his mistress.

When, at line 13, the speaker asserts *Catullus obdurat*, he seems to be speaking *for* "Catullus." The shift from the speaker's earlier mode of addressing "Catullus" to speaking for him implies an attempt, on the speaker's part, to suppress the voice of "Catullus" altogether. However, beginning at line 14, the sudden outburst of emotion directed at the *puella* makes clear that the speaker has, indeed, been unsuccessful in his attempts to control "Catullus." The fact that in line 14, the *puella* switches from being the object (*te*) of the speaker's declaration about "Catullus'" new resolve to being the subject in line 15 (*at tu dolebis*) changes the focus dramatically from viewing the *puella* at a distance to experiencing her once again with passionate emotional involvement.

The outburst that begins at line 14 leads to a series of impassioned questions which shows quite clearly that "Catullus'" obsession with the *puella* is beginning to overpower the speaker's rational appeals. The brief, breathless questions to the mistress about who her new lovers will be, which culminate in the specific images of her kissing and biting another man's lips, demonstrate the extent to which "Catullus'" passion for his mistress is taking over. But here, the imagination of the beloved is quite different from the earlier evocation of past romantic bliss. The voice we now hear in lines 16–19 is that of a man tormented by images of infidelity, compelled to relive the pain of betrayal and rejection. With masochistic pageantry, he trots out the images of his beloved in the arms of potential rivals. It seems now that the voice of firm resolve has virtually left "Catullus," and all attempts to draw away from the beloved have proven to be fruitless and paltry.

The poem does not end, however, with the pathetic outpourings of the abandoned, jealous lover. The sudden, admonishing voice of the speaker interrupts the concern with the *puella*'s infidelity. But the speaker's voice in the last line, as he attempts a last-ditch effort to make reason prevail (*at tu, Catulle, destinatus obdura*) is feeble compared with the frenzied obsession in the speaker's questions about the *puella*. That the speaker begins his admonition of "Catullus" in the last line with the qualifying conjunction *at* reveals that his confidence in his own earlier stance of rationality has been shaken. He is unable to conjure in himself the same degree of resolve he had at the beginning of the poem. The emphatic position of *at* in the last line stresses the ambivalence and confusion inherent in the lover's situation.

Poem 72

In Poems 72 and 76, Catullus once again explores the conflict between the speaker's uncontrollable passion for Lesbia and the rational understanding of the destructiveness of that passion. As in Poem 8, in these poems the speaker attempts to cure himself of his compulsion by using the voice of reason to convince himself that his desire for Lesbia is a disease that will indeed destroy him. But in both poems Catullus associates the desire for Lesbia with the violation of a self-imposed moral code. He frames the speaker's situation in such a way as to make it seem as though he not only suffers from rejection but also from moral degradation in the process. In both poems the connection between uncontrollable desires and moral weakness is not only made more explicit but is also linked more directly to social status and political power. Edwards points out that "those who could not govern themselves, whose desires were uncontrollable" were thought to be unfit to rule the state.[15] Thus the capacity for self-regulation, Edward argues, is crucial if one is to maintain *dignitas* (social standing), without which a man could not negotiate in the world of Roman politics and power relations.

In Poem 72 one of the ways the speaker presents his emotional struggle is by focusing on the disparity between how he and Lesbia perceive their love as well as different ways of loving in general. Through his characteristic manipulation of pronominal forms, Catullus reveals erotic conflict by creating a clear separation between the speaker who uses the first person and "Catullus" to whom the speaker refers in the third person. The poem, however, is addressed to Lesbia, and in the first four lines the speaker states his version of their past love in contrast with hers.

> Dicebas quondam solum te nosse Catullum,
>   Lesbia, nec prae me velle tenere Iovem.
> dilexi tum te non tantum ut vulgus amicam,
>   sed pater ut gnatos diligit et generos.
> 5   nunc te cognovi: quare etsi impensius uror,
>   multo mi tamen es vilior et levior.
> qui potis est, inquis? quod amantem iniuria talis
>   cogit amare magis, sed bene velle minus.

[You used once to say that you were Catullus' only friend, Lesbia, and that you would not prefer Jupiter himself to me. I loved you then, not only as the common sort love a mistress, but as a father loves his sons and sons-in-law. Now I know you; and therefore, though I burn more ardently, yet you are in my sight much less worthy and lighter. How can that be? you say. Because such injury as this drives a lover to be more of a lover, but less of a friend.]

The speaker opens by quoting Lesbia's former words, which explain how she experienced not only their love but "Catullus" himself. However, we have a problem here already. Who is this "Catullus"? Why does the speaker say that Lesbia referred to "Catullus" in the third person? It becomes confusing when the speaker shifts immediately within the first sentence from the third to the first person: *Dicebas quondam solum te nosse Catullum, /Lesbia, nec prae me velle tenere Iovem.* By making a sudden shift from "Catullus" as subject in the first line to "Catullus" as object (*me*) in the second line, we are made aware of the disparity between Lesbia's experience of "Catullus" and the speaker's experience of himself. We will also see in the second half of this poem that the schism between the perspectives of Lesbia and the speaker is the same schism that exists within the speaker himself.

The version of "Catullus" which Lesbia offers is a "Catullus" who is known to her through the experiences conveyed by *nosse* and *tenere,* verbs that clearly bear an erotic physical meaning.[16] In addition, Lesbia's overblown statement that she would, in essence, prefer "Catullus" to Jupiter is an indication of her duplicitousness because it is certainly not Jupiter who rivals "Catullus" for Lesbia's affections. The speaker contradicts Lesbia's understanding of their past relationship by offering an entirely different version of love: *dilexi tum te non tantum ut vulgus amicam* (line 3). Here, the speaker clearly distinguishes love (*dilexi*) that is based on esteem and respect and love that is based on a carnal bond. In the next line, the speaker expands the idea of a nonphysical love by comparing his love for Lesbia with the love of a father for his sons and sons-in-law.[17] The speaker wants Lesbia to know that although his love *includes* physical passion, he considers his spiritual and emotional bond with her to be the more important aspects of his love. Adding *generos* to *gnatos* accentuates the speaker's insistence on the uniqueness of his love for Lesbia because a father's love for his sons-in-law involves no physical bond at all. In addition, including both sons and sons-in-law stresses a community of interest which characterizes the Roman family and stretches out to the politico-familial bonds in the whole of Roman society.

The kind of bond the speaker describes is one from which women were largely excluded. Here the speaker stresses that his love for Lesbia is not the ordinary love of a man for a woman (*ut vulgus amicam*) but that it has more in common with the deepest bonds among men. The effect of such a pronouncement would be to elevate Lesbia far above the ordinary lot of women in that she is worthy of being loved both as a man and as a woman. Putting his private bond with Lesbia in a larger social and moral context sets up a much higher standard of behavior and action than we find, for example, in Poem 8, where the speaker's inability to stop desiring Lesbia remains more of a personal emotional problem. Here, the speaker keeps his passion in bounds by subjugating it to the higher demands of communal, moral obligation and perhaps more importantly by locating his *amor* within the realm of élite male power relations. Saying that he loves Lesbia the way fathers love their sons is to say that he loves her as a "man," that is, with the self-control and indifference to emotional and sexual indulgence expected of a male citizen worthy of *dignitas*.

At line 5, when the speaker announces to Lesbia *nunc te cognovi*, the voice we hear reverberates with the rational awareness implied in the speaker's ability to temper obsessive love with larger moral and intellectual concerns. Moreover, *nunc te cognovi* resonates with other meanings as well. The way in which "Catullus" and Lesbia know one another according to her version of their love (*nosse*) conflicts with "Catullus'" description of their love as primarily spiritual. Her statement to "Catullus" at the beginning shows that her standard for judging their erotic union and for knowing "Catullus" is primarily in terms of physical passion. But, by telling Lesbia that the basis of his love is radically different from hers, "Catullus" reveals to her that he is indeed unlike the "Catullus" she knows.

Despite the speaker's rational awareness of Lesbia's true character, we see that his clear-sighted understanding has no impact whatsoever on how he actually behaves and *feels* toward her. That the speaker burns *more* intensely for Lesbia despite knowing her not only accentuates the irrationality of his desire but also stresses the deep division between the "Catullus" Lesbia experiences and the speaker who is the agent of his own actions, thoughts, and imagination. The speaker reveals the moral dimension of his emotional conflict in line 6 where he calmly tells Lesbia that now that he has seen her real character, his respect for her has diminished considerably: *multo mi tamen es vilior et levior*. We are reminded here of the repulsion expressed toward Lesbia in Catullus' "*odi et amo*" poem. We see now that the speaker's hatred of Lesbia comes not only from her rejection of him but also from what he perceives to be her violation of his moral ideal of a *sancta amicitia*.

The contradiction in the speaker's bald assertion of his increasing desire for Lesbia and diminishing esteem for her elicits the reaction of incredulity from his addressee. Moreover, in the first half of the poem, the speaker presents the discourse of Lesbia and "Catullus" in the narrative past compared with a present moment of discourse, indicated by *nunc te cognovi* at line 5 and *inquis* at line 7. The contrast in how Lesbia and "Catullus" experience knowing (*nosse* and *cognoscere*) is accompanied by the shift from the past to the present. The speaker's movement from narrative to present discourse distances him from the past sufficiently so that he can see both Lesbia and himself from a more rational perspective. The use of *cognoscere* as opposed to *nosse* implies not only that "Catullus" is able to see Lesbia more clearly but that his own powers of rationality are operating and allow him to see and understand his own fragmentation.

At the end of the poem, the speaker's ability to describe his dilemma in general rather than in exclusively personal terms and to abstract a general truth from his own experience reveals a degree of control which contradicts the speaker's presentation of himself as hopelessly divided between what he knows (*cognovi*) and what he feels (*uror*). The very thing the speaker is revealing about himself is his lack of control in being able to carry out the dictates of reason and conscience. The voice we hear in the last line of the poem, however, is not the voice of a man out of control but the voice of self-reflection and profound self-understanding. The paradox that this last line demonstrates so vividly is the way the poet-lover can remove himself from his own personal narrative and see himself whole at the same time that he is powerless to integrate the voices warring within him.

Poem 76

In Poem 76, we see again a speaker addressing a tortured "Catullus" and trying to convince him to stop making himself miserable and to yield to reason. We also see the speaker use moral imperatives in trying to persuade "Catullus" that persistence in his feelings for Lesbia will only lead him further into moral degradation. However, unlike Poems 8 and 72, Poem 76 offers no release whatsoever from the utter helplessness of the lover "Catullus," no sense (or at most, limited) of healing in the poetic act. We have, instead, tortured self-address resolving into even more tortured apostrophes to the gods.

>   Siqua recordanti benefacta priora voluptas
>   est homini, cum se cogitat esse pium,
>   nec sanctam violasse fidem, nec foedere in ullo
>   divum ad fallendos numine abusum homines,
> 5   multa parata manent in longa aetate, Catulle,
>   ex hoc ingrato gaudia amore tibi.
>   nam quaecumque homines bene cuiquam aut dicere possunt
>   aut facere, haec a te dictaque factaque sunt;
>   omnia quae ingratae perierunt credita menti.
> 10 quare cur tu te iam amplius excrucies?
>   quin tu animo offirmas atque istinc teque reducis,
>   dis invitis desinis esse miser?
>   difficile est longum subito deponere amorem.
>   difficile est, verum hoc qualubet efficias:

15 una salus haec est, hoc est tibi pervincendum,
       hoc facias, sive id non pote sive pote.
    o di, si vestrum est misereri, aut si quibus umquam
       extremam iam ipsa in morte tulistis opem,
    me miserum aspicite et, si vitam puriter egi,
20   eripite hanc pestem perniciemque mihi,
    quae mihi subrepens imos ut torpor in artus
       expulit ex omni pectore laetitias.
    non iam illud quaero, contra me ut diligat illa,
       aut, quod non potis est, esse pudica velit:
25 ipse valere opto et taetrum hunc deponere morbum.
       o di, reddite mi hoc pro pietate mea.

[If a man can take any pleasure in recalling the thought of kindnesses done, when he thinks that he has been a true friend; and that he has not broken sacred faith, nor in any compact has used the majesty of the gods in order to deceive men, then there are many joys in a long life for you, Catullus, earned from this thankless love. For whatever kindness human beings can show to one another by word or deed has been said and done by you. All this was entrusted to an ungrateful heart, and is lost: why then should you torment yourself now any more? Why do you not settle your mind firmly, and draw back, and cease to be miserable, in spite of the gods? It is difficult suddenly to lay aside a long-cherished love. It is difficult; but you should accomplish it, one way or another. This is the only safety, this you must carry through, this you are to do, whether it is possible or impossible. Gods, if mercy is your attribute, or if you ever brought aid to any at the very moment of death, look upon me in my trouble, and if I have led a pure life, take away this plague and ruin from me. A lethargy creeping into my inmost joints has cast out all joys from my heart! No longer is this my prayer, that she should love me in return, or, for that is impossible, that she should consent to be chaste. I ask to be well again and to put away this hateful sickness. O gods, grant me this in return for my piety.]

As in Poem 8, the speaker attempts to persuade "Catullus" to stop tormenting himself over the unworthy Lesbia. But here the speaker's strategy is quite different. Rather than merely being the voice of masculine practicality ("it's time to cut your losses, 'Catullus' "), the speaker in 76 attempts to convince "Catullus" logically that his self-torment is not only unreasonable but unnecessary. The speaker offers a specific remedy for "Catullus' " suffering by exhorting him to draw solace from his moral rectitude and the rewards he can expect from it. The speaker uses the strategy of giving "Catullus" what seems to be an air-tight argument in the form of a conditional syllogism. This argument purports to support the idea that "Catullus" will eventually be rewarded for his *pietas* and that he can expect the *multa gaudia* that will come from past *benefacta* to replace his present misery. In addition, part of the speaker's strategy is to divert "Catullus'" attention away from the specificity of his situation and to make him see himself in a larger social and intellectual context. The rewards that "Catullus" will reap are predicated on his collusion in Roman cultural ideals, which will sanctify his past *benefacta* and presumably redeem him from his own misery and degradation by elevating him from private despair to communal validation.

The speaker's seemingly logical argument, however, rests on a rather shaky premise.[18] In the first place, the erotic principles of *fides, sancta amicitia,* and *foedus* are fallacious in light of Lesbia's unfaithfulness and betrayal of her husband.[19] Ironically, what makes Catullus' world of love possible, and, in fact the elegiac world in general, is the violation of law, piety, sanctity, chastity, etc. As we learn explicitly in several of Catullus' poems (notably 5, 7, and 11), Catullus rejects the Roman cultural system and its values; and yet to preserve the seriousness of the erotic world, Catullus must transfer the terms of the world he is rejecting to his own world. The problem is that in order to maintain his personal erotic ideal, Catullus must preserve the illusion that the elegiac world is the real world. Poem 76 dramatizes the extent to which the two worlds are in conflict by showing the impossibility of incorporating Roman cultural values into the private world of the lover.

The fact that the speaker in 76 is completely ineffectual in his attempts to console the lover by invoking the primary standards of validation for the self shows how those standards simply are not applicable to the lover's experience. The speaker's argument culminates with a series of questions to "Catullus" which imply the logical inevitability of "Catullus" being able to change his miserable state: "You ought to be able to take pleasure in the knowledge that you have been *pius,* and that knowledge ought to console you in your misery, so why do you continue to torment yourself?" "Catullus'" answer to the speaker's questions (*difficile est longum subito deponere amorem*) exposes the fallacy in the speaker's argument. "Catullus" simply does not *feel* any pleasure in recalling his past *benefacta,* nor does he get any real validation of himself from applying Roman standards of value to his own experience. The lover simply feels the way he does, and there is nothing he can *do* about it. The impasse the speaker reaches in getting through to "Catullus" leads him to the strategy of suggesting the impossible. Although he acknowledges "Catullus'" difficulty, the speaker resorts to a desperate power move in commanding him to take action whether it is possible for him or not (*hoc facias, sive id non pote sive pote*, line 16).

Compared with the firm, resolute voice of the speaker in Poem 8, here the speaker's voice resonates with confusion and tentativeness. His illogic, the conditional nature of his argument, and the fact that initially, he uses questions rather than imperatives to convince "Catullus" to stop tormenting himself, all support an impression of the speaker as irresolute and uncertain. At line 15, we begin to feel the voices of the speaker and the lover "Catullus" merge as the speaker's desperation forces him to shift his strategy from using logic to move "Catullus" to appealing to "Catullus" emotionally by making his change a matter of life and death (*una salus haec est*). The speaker is as helpless to change "Catullus" as "Catullus" is to change himself; their mutual desperation draws them together. The speaker abandons his own logical discourse and begins to speak in the more emotional language of the tormented lover. The speaker's sudden shift from second person to first person to request help from the gods on "Catullus'" behalf reinforces a sense of confusion about who is speaking—the frenzied lover or the calm, rational speaker.

The whole prayer, in fact, is a conflation of the two voices of speaker and lover. On the one hand, the conditional form in the opening of the prayer naturally recalls the speaker's conditional sentences in his argument to "Catullus" at the beginning of the poem. On the other hand, we hear the voice of the lover "Catullus" in the desperate plea to the gods to have pity on a wretched man on the brink of death. The whole invocation vacillates between the points of view of speaker and lover. The fact that the invocation is predicated on a false argument, one that clearly does not apply to the situation of the lover because it is based on logical premises, falsifies both voices we hear in the prayer to the gods. If the speaker is speaking on behalf of "Catullus" as he does in Poem 8, then he is not taking into account the falseness of his own argument and the futility of applying his standards to the private world of the lover. Also false is "Catullus" speaking this prayer because he uses an argument whose validity his own experience contradicts. Clearly, it would be extremely difficult for the lover "Catullus" to believe in an argument that is predicated on the conviction that values of piety and moral virtue are what matter. The lover knows he cannot change the way he feels, no matter how illogical it may be. "Catullus'" disclaimer about no longer wanting Lesbia's love or her chastity is only further proof that he is incapable of drawing away from her. No matter how irrational, the lover will always harbor eleventh-hour possibilities for reunion with the beloved.

Although the lover expresses a wish to be healthy and to be rid of a love he calls a *taetrum morbum*,[20] his emotionality and helplessness at the end render such an eventuality doubtful. The speaker's use of *deponere* in line 24 to express his wish for the gods to "put away" his sickness echoes his earlier use of *deponere* in line 13, where he expresses his hopelessness about his ability to overcome his *longum amorem*. Although the speaker reaches the same impasse here as he does in other poems, the difference is that he does not merely accept his fragmentation as an inevitable and irreparable fact of his condition. In Poems 8 and 72 Catullus clearly delineates the voices of speaker and lover and preserves the conflict between them. But the speaker's voice in 76, as he makes his emotional plea to the gods to cure him of his "sickness" in return for his piety, encompasses the perspectives and the discourses of both speaker and lover. The admission of helplessness implied in the appeal to the gods as well as the speaker's frenzied emotional tone express the lover's characteristically wretched condition. But the speaker's expression of hope that his piety may ultimately bring him "health" implies a belief in the possibility that a commitment to virtue can prevail over uncontrollable passion. The speaker's earlier advice to "Catullus" to "cure" himself of his irrational love by consoling himself with his past *benefacta* is incorporated into the speaker's emotional plea to the gods. By collapsing the voices of speaker and lover into one another in this way, Catullus suggests that the solution to erotic conflict may at least begin with the awareness that the lover's frenzy is a sickness. Moreover, through the speaker's suggestion that an adherence to traditional Roman ideals may enable the lover to get over his irrational passion, Catullus expresses the hope that the lover's ability to see himself as part of a larger social context *may* be a cure for his private anguish.

The radical antagonism in Catullus' lyric consciousness culminates most dramatically in the speaker's effort to master his private feelings by gaining valorization from the public world. At the end of Poem 76, the multivoiced Catullan poetic *ego* seems hopelessly tangled up in the oppositional discourses of the private and public worlds. The speaker's inability to identify adequately with either form of discourse makes it difficult to attach the Catullan *ego* to a clearly defined narrative or set of meanings. Indeed, as W. R. Johnson observes, Catullus' complex multilayered consciousness that culminates in Poem 76 reveals a lyric subjectivity new to Western literature:

> what was merely troublesome in Poem 8 becomes, in Poem 76, a disease that has devoured the personality. To write about oneself and one's life, that was not new; but to write about inner conflicts and divisions, about the fragmentations of self that could barely be glimpsed, never truly understood; to try to grasp these opaque inward alienations and to dramatize the attempts

to grasp them—that was, very probably, new for lyric poetry. The monodist has now discovered that beneath the singing, writing self there are many selves, many wills.[21]

Although Catullus does not reconcile those "many selves" in his poetry, he identifies them in a complex set of relations to one another which defies reduction to any unitary discursive practice or experience of the self. Catullus' poetic discourse does not reconstitute the fragmentation of the lover, but it embodies—with intense clarity—the contradictions and incompletion inherent in the condition of desire itself.

CHAPTER TWO

Gendered Domains
Public and Private in Catullus

*C*ATULLUS' ANDROGYNOUS poetic voice, which characterizes desire as a complex configuration of gender identities, may suggest that desire itself is degendering. In the previous chapter we saw how desire in Catullus confounds traditional categories of gender. When the Catullan lover speaks as a desiring subject, he cannot do so in a voice that is exclusively male or female. Yet in a number Catullus' poems, the narrator explicitly dissociates himself from cultural practices, attitudes, and values that are traditionally regarded and delimited as male. In other words, the realm of public and political activity from which women were formally excluded is the very realm to which the Catullan lover often opposes himself. The complexity of gender categories in poems that express the most conflict in the lover's attitudes toward Lesbia also comes to the fore, though perhaps more subtly, in poems in which the lover seems to dichotomize public and private realms — poems where the lover embraces his personal passions in flagrant opposition to the public and political life, as in Poems 5, 7, and, as I will argue, in Poem 11 as well.

A curious feature of many of the Lesbia poems is the confusion engendered by the speaker's attribution of the name *Lesbia* as a pseudonym for his mistress and his tendency to associate Lesbia with certain masculine traits that are identified with a scheme of values the speaker derogates. On the one hand, the name *Lesbia* evokes a Sapphic world of beauty, imagination, and *feminine* desire. On the other hand, this same Lesbia is designated as a part of a corrupt (masculine) world of commercialism and conquest. These conflicting views of Lesbia may, on one level, be said to reflect traditional male stereotypes of the woman as either Goddess or Whore.[1]

But, as usual in Catullus, easy dichotomies break down. The separation of the real from the ideal—the attempt to create an idealized world of love undisrupted or untainted by the degradation of Roman mercantilist values—is shown to be unstable at best. Lesbia, I shall argue, is, despite her name, never a Goddess, never a figure of Sapphic beauty and desire. Even in the lover's most rapturous moments, Lesbia is never excluded from the exterior world that the speaker vehemently devalues. And in the lover's most disappointed, angry moments, Lesbia becomes a caricature of all that is wrong with the world; the Catullan lover reads himself into Lesbia at every turn.[2] When the lover confidently asserts his ideal of living a life of passion and imagination in the face of the hostile stares of censorious old men, Lesbia is merely a *causa* for the speaker's ecstatic denial of practical reality. She herself lags behind in mundane nontranscendence. Or, to put it another way, she seems to lack any desire of her own; her role is to enable the speaker's "mad" desire. And when the speaker rails at Lesbia for her alleged infidelities, she becomes a monstrous projection of the speaker's hatred toward women in general.

Catullus' appropriation of the feminine through his adoption of a feminine persona and through his apparent rejection of conventional masculine values is not, I believe, only an instance of the male poet "playing the other" or revealing the destructive effects on the male personality of polarized gender roles.[3] Rather, Catullus' adoption of a feminine persona and his attendant hostility to traditional Roman male attitudes and practices paradoxically reinforce conventional male attitudes about power and, particularly, about establishing a moral hierarchy in which men are viewed as superior to women. As Elaine Showalter remarks, "mastery of the feminine has long been a stance of masculine authority."[4]

In this chapter, I shall discuss three poems that epitomize Catullus' attitudes toward the public domain: 5, 7, and 11. In these three poems Catullus expresses what seem to be conflicting positions about traditional male cultural discourses and practices. I will interrogate those conflicting attitudes in light of Catullus' inversion of gender roles in the hope of elucidating the ways that gender ideology is inscribed, represented, and reproduced in poems that explicitly address or use the public domain as a focal point of self-definition for the speaker. Furthermore, I want to explore the paradoxical figure of Lesbia as a vehicle, on the one hand, for the speaker's antimasculine ideal, and, on the other hand, for his stereotypically misogynistic attitudes.

Poems 5 and 7

Although we hear a tortured, embattled voice in Catullus' self-addressing poems, as we saw in Chapter 1 it is not the only voice in his erotic poems about Lesbia. In Poem 11 and in Poems 5 and 7 where he joyfully addresses Lesbia and exclaims about their blissfully transcendent union, the poet-lover makes a clear distinction between his own erotic ideal of purity and sincerity and the world's degradation. In these poems, the speaker is turned outward from himself, confidently regarding the world with irony and scorn and, at the same time, having enough clarity of self-presentation to look at the way the world sees him. These are moments in which Catullus' poetic voice attempts to prevail over a world that threatens to nullify erotic experience as a viable way of being in the world.

In these poems, especially in 11, the situation remains one of erotic frustration, alienation, or, at best, misunderstanding. Lesbia is represented as an adversary the speaker can either destroy or win over with his poetic prowess. She is always, to some degree, separate from the speaker's imaginative, erotic life. She remains part of the world and is always associated with the values from which Catullus constantly tries to separate himself. Poems 5 and 7 are generally regarded as the only erotic poems of Catullus in which the narrator is not divided in his feelings toward his mistress. In these poems, we see a poet-lover who is not obsessed with his own internal drama but who exuberantly uses his poetic prowess to defend the imaginative, erotic life and to defeat a mechanized world that threatens to devalue that life.

Although in Poems 5 and 7, the speaker exclaims joyfully about his union with Lesbia, she nonetheless remains at a distance from the world Catullus offers as an alternative to the mercantile world of Roman society. Even in Poem 5, Lesbia is not quite fully at one with Catullus' blissful, erotic ideal. The speaker must either ask for erotic fulfillment or persuade and reassure Lesbia of the worth of his erotic ideal.

> Vivamus, mea Lesbia, atque amemus
> rumoresque senum severiorum
> omnes unius aestimemus assis.
> soles occidere et redire possunt:

nobis cum semel occidit brevis lux,
nox est perpetua una dormienda.
da mi basia mille, deinde centum,
dein mille altera, dein secunda centum,
deinde usque altera mille, deinde centum
dein, cum milia multa fecerimus,
conturbabimus illa, ne sciamus,
aut nequis malus invidere possit,
cum tantum sciat esse basiorum.

[Let us live, my Lesbia, and let us love,
and value at one cent the talk of crabby old men.
Suns may set and rise again.
For us, once the brief light has set,
night is one continuous sleep.
Give me a thousand kisses, then a hundred,
then another thousand, then a second hundred,
then yet another thousand, then a hundred.
Then, when we have made many thousands,
we will confuse our counting, so that we may not
know, nor will anyone be able to cast an evil eye,
when he knows that our kisses are so many.]⁵

Poem 5 opens with a bold declaration of power, the first line framed by a double command—a far cry from the anguish we hear in many of Catullus' poems of self-address. The speaker joins life and love in the first line and suggests that life worth living is, for him, a matter of passion. The fact that *mea Lesbia* is contained within *vivamus* and *amemus* suggests that the acts of living and loving are dependent on the speaker's possession of his beloved. However, even though the speaker addresses the poem to Lesbia, he immediately turns his attention to the crabby old men who disapprove of the passionate life that he so confidently advocates.

The speaker cleverly dismisses these conservative, upstanding members of Roman society by answering them in their own terms and evaluating them according to their own standards. By applying monetary values to human worth, the speaker not only dismisses them but also negates the world to which they belong, which makes money—numerical quantification—the primary means of human exchange and validation. By exposing the absurdity of rendering human worth accountable, the speaker transvalues the mechanism of accounting altogether. Moreover, numerical reckoning is made to seem small and petty in the larger context of the eternal cycles of nature, the rising and setting of the sun. However, it is the use of quantification discourse which makes the speaker aware of limits. Neither the lovers nor the *senes* can escape the *brevis lux* of human life. The speaker's vibrant and energetic voice at the beginning of the poem begins to sober and darken, a harbinger of death rather than an exclaimer of the joys of erotic experience.

The urgency with which the poet-lover makes his entreaty of Lesbia and the sudden intrusion of repeated imperatives into the somber mood of lines 6 and 7 shake up the sense of limitation which is conveyed in the images of death and accounting. The languid torpor of *dormienda* followed by the sharply immediate sound of *da* awakens us back into life and out of the sober contemplation of death. Both death and numerical accounting create the stasis of affixing absolute meaning and definition to things. It is that external imposition of meaning and order to which the speaker reacts in line 7, when he attempts to overturn the bounds of order and decorum in his passionate request for so many kisses.

In his essay "Catullus 5 and 7: A Study in Complementaries," Charles Segal points out how Catullus' seemingly "wild, passionate jumble" of numbers actually occurs in an orderly succession. He shows how the repetition of *centum* at the end of each line, *deinde centum* at the end of the first and third lines, as well as the repetition of *mille* in all three lines enforces an impression of order and control. Segal also shows, however, that the primal, monosyllabic simplicity of Catullus' language here mirrors the "passionate gestures of the lover" and that "the poet himself enacts that reckless scorn of society and sober opinion which he advocated in the opening lines."[6] Although Catullus uses numerical reckoning in these lines, his use of repetition has a mesmerizing effect that contradicts the practical, controlled discourse of the commercial world. The speaker's passionate, hypnotic expression of love's power refuses to acknowledge limits, refuses to acknowledge the power that the world has over the lovers. The world, momentarily, is blotted out, and all that exists is the energy generated by the lover's kisses, which have no practical use in the world but exist as an end in themselves. What gets confused and jumbled up is not only the number of the lovers' kisses but the meaning and importance of the accounting principle itself. Not only do the lovers become confused by their number of kisses, but the mixing of the languages of love and money confounds the narrow expectations of the old men. The *mali*'s rigid understanding of the world in quantifiable and material terms is thrown into disarray by the clever hyperbolizing of the poet-lover. Suddenly, the world of the *mali* does not make sense in the context of love. The speaker not only exposes the bankruptcy of their world beyond the narrow sphere of its own limited terms, he also shows how the calculative impulse is itself a kind of death, a way of making things static, frozen in meaning and possibility. The juxtaposition of the *rumores* of the *senes*, valued at one cent (*unius assis*), and the one night (*una dormienda*) of death suggests that death and numerical calculation are equally limiting.

As Portia defeats Shylock in *The Merchant of Venice*, the poet-lover defeats the old men by making love learn to speak the public language. The rigidity and limits of the discourse of public and practical affairs are exposed, not by abandoning that discourse but by exploiting it fully. The speaker's passionate exclaiming of numbers defies arithmetic even as it puts it to full use. Catullus shows us how numerical reckoning leads only to the one night of death and can never overcome the constraints of time. Only by using the structures of numerical calculation can the speaker destroy them. The poem itself, like the numbers, is the container that embodies limit and control and transcends it at the same time.

The operations of knowing (*sciat* and *sciamus*) have, by being carried to ludicrous extremes, been rendered both useless and powerless to defy the inevitable sleep of death. The limits set by numerical calculation, by the rational knowledge of things, are overturned in the speaker's transgression of numerical restraints. By the end of the poem, neither the lovers nor the *malus* knows how many kisses the lovers have had. The cleverness of Catullus' strategy here is reinforced by the way he confuses us about who knows what. He tells us at the end that the lovers will not know (*ne sciamus*) how many kisses they have made (*fecerimus*) and that the *malus* will know (*sciat*) that the lovers' kisses are so many. The speaker has succeeded in rendering the *mali*'s attempts at calculation powerless. By employing the limiting and predictable structures of rational discourse in his cleverly jumbled use of *scire*, the speaker makes the rational, calculatory modes of operation of the *mali* subservient to the discourse of passion—in which finite, arithmetic calculations explode into the realm of the incalculable and unknowable.

Although the speaker formally addresses Lesbia in the poem, his focus of attention from the beginning is on the shadowy presence of the *mali* whose hostile gaze and incomprehending perspective threaten to destroy the passionate happiness of the lovers. In fact, these censorious old men are not merely the conservative and practical members of Roman society, they also symbolize values of commercialism according to which life is hoarded, reined in, and understood by the calculations of bureaucratic record keeping. It is to these men and the values they embody that the poet-lover really addresses his poem. The apostrophe to Lesbia is merely a dramatic means of asserting the claims of the passionate life. Lesbia's presence is swept up in the passionate exchange of kisses, in the urgency to defeat the long sleep of death. The drama is not so much in the erotic moment as it is in the conflict between the clashing modes of public and private discourse. The object of desire is subordinated to the urgent need of the narrator's poetic voice to exclaim more potently than the old men do in their malicious talk (*rumores*).

What does the speaker mean when he entreats Lesbia to "let us love"? Is he merely asking her to be his accomplice in living the passionate life, or does his bold exhortation to devalue the crabby opinions of the *mali* suggest Lesbia's overriding concern for their values and her inability to participate fully with the speaker in pursuing exultantly the erotic life? Are her hesitation and concern for the opinions and values of the *mali* suggested in the speaker's reassurance to her that the *rumores* of the old men are worth nothing at all? I think so. I would argue that the address to Lesbia here comes out of the need to persuade her as much as out of the need to express his disdain for the valuation embodied in the calculating gazes of the *mali*. In fact, the narrator does not imagine the consummation of his union with Lesbia. He merely asks Lesbia for kisses in so passionate and confident a way that we cannot help but imagine that his request will be fulfilled. But there is nothing in the poem which conjures up erotic fulfillment. Rather than Lesbia's presence being felt, the speaker's request for kisses takes on a life of its own. His passionate utterance of unmediated desire (*da*) in its expression of "infinite potency and energy" seems to stand on its own, an end in itself rather than a means to the imaginative re-creation of ideal, erotic union. The speaker's desire to outstrip the bounds of bureaucratic orderliness and transcend the infinitely limiting fact of death instigates the urgency of his passionate exclamation of desire for Lesbia.

Despite his formal apostrophe to her, the speaker's concern is not directed toward Lesbia here but rather toward the evil eyes of death and the *mali*. In his clever defeat of both, the poet-lover not only achieves the triumph of his personal ideal; more subtly, he subdues Lesbia by subordinating her completely to his imaginative vision, by proving to her that the world with which she is consistently identified is inherently impotent. We see this theme repeated throughout the majority of his poems about Lesbia. In Poem 7, where the speaker also requests infinite kisses that will confound the *curiosi,* one can detect not only that Lesbia is a catalyst (rather than a mutual participant) for the speaker's unbounded desire but that she is associated more explicitly with the world of the *curiosi*.[7] Indeed, that Lesbia requires quantification does seem to align her more with the materialistic values so prevalent in Roman culture

—those very values Catullus seems to scorn. Moreover, because the speaker is addressing Lesbia when he refers to himself as "mad Catullus," one can infer that Catullus' passion and his imaginative flights from the mundane and practical seem as "mad" to Lesbia as to the crotchety, evil-tongued *curiosi*.

The overall impression that emerges in both 5 and 7 is that the speaker and his mistress are in different—if not opposite—camps. The male lover is clearly portrayed as on a higher moral plane than his number-crunching mistress, whose ability to go beyond *material* concerns is very limited. Such a view of the woman evokes male stereotypes about women as creatures hopelessly doomed by their sex to dwell in the realm of nature, of *matter*. As the feminist theorist Judith Butler observes, the classical association of woman with materiality can be traced to a set of etymologies in which *materia* (matter) is linked with *mater*.[8] Indeed, for Aristotle, it is women who contribute form in reproduction and men who impose form or actuality on the potentiality of matter.[9] In her book *Sowing the Body*, Page duBois points out that the image of woman as a "field-to-be-ploughed" is one of the most stereotypical metaphors used for women in Greek culture. Her analysis of the metaphors linking the female body with the earth in representations of women in Greek literature and art reveals the ways in which the identification of femaleness with nature is embedded deeply in the Western tradition.[10]

In Poems 5 and 7, the association of Lesbia with material and practical concerns and the identification of the male lover with an ideal realm of beauty and imagination reinforce traditional gender polarities and hierarchies. The sphere associated with femininity and nature has traditionally been accorded lower value than that associated with masculinity and freedom.[11] In Poem 5, Lesbia's implicit identification with the circumscribed, mercantile world of the *mali* compared with the narrator's imaginary flight into the realm of the incalculable reinforces a moral asymmetry associated with traditional gender division. "In the mythical text, then," de Lauretis writes, "the hero must be male regardless of the gender of the character, because the obstacle . . . is morphologically female—and indeed, simply, the womb, the earth, the space of his movement."[12] Indeed, in Poems 5 and 7, though more explicitly in 7, Lesbia personifies the "resistance," the boundary the speaker crosses to move through time and space. In both 5 and 7, the Catullan lover speaks with magisterial authority; in 5, the opening phrase "Let us live, let us love" establishes a tone of absolute authority which is reinforced by the speaker's demonstrations of mobility through and beyond mortal limits; in 7, the speaker denies limits by traversing vast expanses of space and moving from the real to the imaginary. It is the woman who, as Janan says, "ineluctably pulls the request back from infinity by asking Catullus to number infinity."[13] Thus, despite the lover's grandiose, passionate expressions of desire for his mistress, she nonetheless represents, at best, *limit,* what is calculable and therefore what must be transcended. At worst, as Poem 11 shows, Lesbia is derided as a horrid monster whose crass values of commercialism come to represent the most degraded aspects of Roman culture.

Poem 11

Poem 11 is one of Catullus' most problematic. Indeed, sorting through the maze of conflicting interpretations about the poem points up the many ambiguities and complexities the poem presents to critics.[14] The most vexing aspect of the poem concerns the speaker's relationship to the public life, marked in the poem by his apparently laudatory attitude toward imperial conquest and toward a life Ernst Fredricksmeyer characterizes as "devoted to strenuous exertions with his male companions in a spirit of friendship, patriotism, and religious respect; in short, a life of *virtus,* as opposed to his past life which had become, through Lesbia, sordid."[15] Fredricksmeyer acknowledges and even enumerates in the Appendix to his article the vast majority of scholars who believe Catullus' attitude toward his *comites* Furius and Aurelius (and Caesar) ought to be taken as ironic. Nonetheless, Fredricksmeyer argues against such an interpretation and asserts that we ought to "interpret the poem by its own evidence." He believes that this evidence shows that "while Lesbia, his *'puella,'* had been Catullus' friend, she is now his enemy, and while Furius and Aurelius had been his enemies, they are now his friends. With this reversal of relationships, Catullus has turned around his life."[16] Fredricksmeyer builds his interpretation around a dichotomy of allegiances; Catullus *now* embraces the masculine world of adventure and action and repudiates his former life of private passion—associated with passive, feminine indulgence. I believe such a dichotomy in the speaker's attitudes and allegiances cannot be marked out so clearly in this poem. I do, however, agree that we ought to try to make sense of the poem on its own terms rather than in relation to the rest of the *corpus.* My reading of the poem will attempt to do that, but I shall argue that the poem expresses a deep ambivalence toward public and private domains and the associations of gender attached to those domains.

In Poem 11, even though Catullus addresses Furius and Aurelius, the thrust of the poem's apostrophe is to Lesbia, in formal terms—the exact reverse of the situation in Poem 5. Poem 11, however, like 5 and 7, implicates Lesbia in a corrupt exterior world. But in 11, the speaker vilifies Lesbia far more than he does the *mali* and *curiosi* and the values they represent. Indeed, one of the most confusing features of Poem 11 is the speaker's identification, on the one hand, with traditional Roman values—which include imperial conquest and the subjugation of others—and, on the other hand, his rejection of Lesbia based on activities that invite comparison with those of both Caesar and his putative *comites*. On Fredricksmeyer's reading, the opposition between the *virtus* of the speaker's male comrades (including Caesar) and the sordidness of Lesbia is unambiguous. The problem with that interpretation is that the supposed moral superiority of living the life of an upright Roman male citizen is undercut in the poem by the linkages between the activities of Lesbia and those of Caesar.

If the speaker wants to condemn Lesbia's depraved conduct, then why does he implicitly draw a parallel between her actions and those of Caesar—actions he supposedly celebrates? I would like to propose an interpretation of the poem which does not look to other poems for an ironic reading but does account for Catullus' contradictory attitudes toward Lesbia's "sordid" conduct and the conduct of both Caesar and Catullus' fellow-travelers. In other words, how can a mode of conduct which involves the subjugation and dehumanization of others be praised in the case of Caesar and condemned in the case of Lesbia? Such a contradiction undermines Fredricksmeyer's view that the speaker, with no irresolution whatsoever, simply renounces his past and embraces a future life of adventure and action.

The inconsistency in the speaker's attitudes toward a life of conquest and "manly exertion" (exhibited by Lesbia in the poem no less than Caesar) points up a continuity of desire which governs both public and private domains—in Rome's imperial conquests and in Lesbia's erotic conquests. Moreover, the confusion of gender distinctions may be linked to a blurring of the boundaries between public and private spheres. Catullus creates the appearance of a male-identified lover who embraces a life of *virtus* and its attendant valorization of "pride as a patriotic citizen in the expansion of the empire."[17] But in the lover's vilification of conquest in the erotic sphere, Catullus points up the monstrosity of conquest as a way of life when taken to the extremes of both Caesar and Lesbia. It is only when we see how rapacious imperialism and unbounded sexual desire are inextricably linked that we are able to see that the speaker's repugnance toward Lesbia also implies a dismissal of the traditional Roman values embodied in the manly exploits of both Caesar and the speaker's "devoted," "faithful" companions. The final identification of the lover with the traditional sign of feminine sexuality (the *flos*) is, I believe, the culminating gesture of alienation not only from masculine identity but also from the excesses and moral bankruptcy of Roman culture. Indeed, I hope to show in my reading of the poem that the activities of *both* Caesar and Lesbia are devalued by the speaker and that the speaker locates himself on the margins of culture — at the edge of the meadow.

> Furi et Aureli, comites Catulli,
> sive in extremos penetrabit Indos,
> litus ut longe resonante Eoa
> 4   tunditur unda,
>
> sive in Hyrcanos Arabasve molles
> seu Sagas sagittiferosque Parthos,
> sive quae septemgeminus colorat
> 8   aequora Nilus,
>
> sive trans altas gradietur Alpes,
> Caesaris visens monimenta magni,
> Gallicum Rhenum, horribilisque ulti-
> 12   mosque Britannos,
>
> omnia haec, quaecumque feret voluntas
> caelitum, temptare simul parati,
> pauca nuntiate meae puellae
> 16   non bona dicta.
>
> cum suis vivat valeatque moechis,
> quos simul complexa tenet trecentos,
> nullum amans vere, sed identidem
> 20   omnium ilia rumpens:
>
> nec meum respectet, ut ante, amorem,
> qui illius culpa cecidit velut prati
> ultimi flos, praetereunte postquam
> 24   tactus aratro est.

[Furius and Aurelius, companions of Catullus, whether he will penetrate into the farthest Indi, where the shore is beaten by the far-resounding Eastern wave, or into the Hyrcani or the soft Arabians, whether to the Sagae or arrow-bearing Parthians, whether into the waters which sevenfold Nile dyes, whether he will cross over the lofty Alps, viewing the memorials of mighty Caesar, the Gallic Rhine, the horrible and remotest Britons — all these things, prepared to test together, whatever the will of the gods shall bring: announce a few words to my girl, words not pleasant. Let her live and flourish with her adulterers, whom three hundred at once she holds in her embrace, loving no one of them truly, but again and again breaking the strength of all. And let her not look, as before, at my love, which by her fault has fallen like a flower of the remotest meadow after it has been touched by a passing plow.]

In Poem 5 it is quite clear who Catullus' enemies are and what his relationship to the exterior world is, but in Poem 11 the situation is far more ambiguous. Like Poem 5, Poem 11 is one of dismissal; however, whom Catullus is dismissing in 11 is not clear. Fredricksmeyer takes at face value the speaker's address to Furius and Aurelius as his devoted friends and his celebration of a life of adventure and action symbolized by the allusion to the grandiose accomplishments of Rome. A close look at the geographical catalogue in lines 1–12 will reveal, however, that the speaker does not offer unequivocal praise either of his *comites* or of the fruits of "manly exertion."

In the very first line of the poem Catullus employs one of his characteristic techniques for demonstrating self-division. Referring to himself in the third person (*comites Catulli*), Catullus makes clear a disparity between the speaker and this "Catullus" who is closely associated with Furius and Aurelius and their exotic travels. In her discussion of the poem, Eve Adler makes the point that when Catullus speaks of himself in the third person, it bears witness to his sense of being seen by others in an incomplete or false way and often suggests an impulse to correct others' views of him.[18] We saw a similar situation in Poem 72 where "Catullus," by using the third-person reference to himself, attempts to correct Lesbia's view of him as someone who is known to her only through the vulgar lens of carnal attraction (*Dicebas quondam solum te nosse Catullum*). Here, the narrator refers to himself in the third person until line 15, where he shifts to the first person.

Adler believes that the "Catullus" of lines 1–14 is the version of Catullus seen by Furius and Aurelius and that, at line 15, the speaker dismisses not only them and their world of travel and conquest but he also repudiates the "Catullus" who is so closely allied with their world and their values. Adler's point is that in lines 15–24, Catullus reveals his true self, a self for whom nothing matters (not all the journeys with Furius and Aurelius) but the loss of what meant most to him: the love of Lesbia. Adler's argument, however, does not account for the more subtle and clever strategies of dismissal which permeate the first half of the poem.

The world that the speaker identifies with Furius and Aurelius and "Catullus" is consummately Roman. In language evoking epic grandeur, the speaker imagines the three *comites* in a wide sweep of geographical locales that all relate to the establishment of the power of Rome—power that from the beginning of the poem is clearly located in the masculine realm. The speaker links "Catullus" to Furius and Aurelius through their shared participation in a life of action. Fredricksmeyer comments on the way Catullus characterizes his future life with his male comrades: "The *ethos* of male friendship, patriotic interest, and religious respect will mark Catullus' attitude in his pursuit of the active life of *virtus*, and this life is the leitmotif of the address to Furius and Aurelius."[19] However, the fact that the speaker in the poem refers to himself in the third person when he is identifying himself with the *vita activa* of Roman citizens suggests that he is removed from such an approach to life. I do not think, as Adler suggests, that the speaker's rejection of "Catullus" begins at line 15 or that the speaker's ironic attitude toward his *comites* only becomes clear once we have read the second half of the poem. I believe that there are hints, in the opening catalogue, of a devaluation and dismissal of the alliance of "Catullus" with Furius and Aurelius and of the values of Roman *virtus* associated with them.

The speaker's description of the friendship between "Catullus" and his comrades seems hyperbolic. The journey the speaker imagines Furius and Aurelius will undertake with "Catullus" is one that is beyond normal human capacity. In their reading of the poem, Blodgett and Nielsen also emphasize the highly exaggerated quality of the way the speaker characterizes the devotion of Furius and Aurelius to "Catullus" which makes a mockery of their friendship: "Friendship and love become something odd, something grotesque, and also, through the use of hyperbole, something impossible to achieve.... No one, as several critics have argued elsewhere, would undertake such a trip (for any purpose). It is proposed because of its very impossibility."[20]

In addition, Blodgett and Nielsen make the intriguing point that the journey described in the catalogue seems not only impossible but also erratic and purposeless and, moreover, that it appears to have no connection with the speaker's message for Lesbia. Although he speaks in epic language to describe the journey with his comrades, the illogic and lack of purpose of that language contradict the normal association of epic with a nobility and clarity of purpose. If the speaker does not want his audience to read the trip literally, if it is rather "a rhetorical journey that is conjured out of nowhere," then what is its purpose in the poem?

I think there is an analogy here between the way the images of distant lands and peoples take on a life of their own, disconnected from real life, and the way the images of *basia mille* in Poem 5 exist as an end in themselves. In both poems, the poet's escape through images provides some release from disappointment and suffering. In Poem 5, the speaker's enemies are the hostile *mali* whose mercantile approach to life threatens to negate his erotic and imaginative impulses. Here, the motif of travel can be understood as the speaker's attempt to flee the agonies of love, to free himself from Lesbia's monstrous grip, and to escape into poetic images.[21] But it is not only the impossibility and lack of purpose of the trip in practical terms which make the images in the catalogue call attention to themselves as poetry. The exotic sensuousness of the description of foreign lands and the erotic undertones also suggest the poet's escape from passion into the realm of imagination.

One can argue that many of the images in the speaker's geographical catalogue contain elements of *eros*.[22] The hypnotic repetition of *sive* conjures a dizzying spectrum of possibilities which expresses a mood of optimism and passion. In general, the images of turbulent, overflowing water in lines 3 and 4 have an erotic quality that disrupts the speaker's apparent identification with imperial Roman values.[23] Indeed, desire shoots through the landscape, creating what Janan calls "another axis of orientation besides that of space."[24] However, the first verb in the poem, *penetrabit* (line 2), may suggest sexual activity and thus evoke male sexual aggression. As the images in the catalogue reveal, the landscape of travel is one of conquest embodied in the *monimenta* erected by Caesar. The images of venturing into the farthest Indi and crossing over the lofty Alps suggest a transgressive crossing of boundaries (*penetrabit*, *gradietur*). Implications of sexual violation become conjoined to unbounded imperialistic conquest; both male sexual prowess and martial conquest ensure and consolidate masculine identity and authority. The speaker, at least on the surface, identifies himself with vigorous manly activity that links him with Caesar's own exploits. But there is confusion in that identification.

As I discussed earlier, the speaker describes the hypothetical journey with his putative comrades as both hyperbolic and erratic. The description itself possesses a transgressive character—a sense that the speaker is carried away by his own grandiose images of travel. Thus, I would argue that the speaker is not, as Fredricksmeyer suggests, giving up his former life of love and imagination for the sake of a life of "friendship, patriotism, and religious respect." The geographical catalogue in lines 1–12 seems more like an imaginative flight that allows the speaker to cross boundaries of time and space—similar to his transgression of numerical restraints in Poem 5. Furthermore, the specific places alluded to in the hypothetical journey reinforce the speaker's alienation from Roman culture. Not only are the Arabians and the *Hyrcani* enemies of Rome, but both the *Arabae* and the *Hyrcani* were associated with Oriental effeminacy.[25] Identifying himself with such places, both geographically (i.e., on the Roman frontier) and culturally, suggests that the speaker positions himself at a distance from the life of (manly) Roman virtue he appears to embrace.

Describing the shared exploits of the three *comites* as *omnia haec* in line 13 turns the specificity of places and activities into a mass of indeterminate "things"—a move suggesting a devaluation whereby the exotic sites of travel and conquest named previously become nameless and unimportant relative to the *pauca* that follow in line 15. The *pauca*, as we soon see, are not really *pauca* at all. The speaker's request to Furius and Aurelius to face a monster such as Lesbia sounds far more terrifying than any of the risks he describes in their journey together. The effect here is not merely to highlight Lesbia's immense power and the frightening danger she poses but to supplant the monumentality of Caesar's world and its concerns with the challenges of the speaker's private world of love. When the speaker abandons his third-person reference to "Catullus" and shifts into the first person, he repudiates not only the exterior, objective world to which both Caesar and Lesbia belong, but he also distances himself, more explicitly than in his catalogue, from any identification with that world.

After more than three stanzas of highly rhetorical, poetic language, the harsh sound of *non bona dicta* in line 16 is startling. Moreover, it is the first full stop in the poem and sets us up for an invective to follow. The style and diction of the invective stanza are, for the most part, in accord with the epic tone of the preceding stanzas. The speaker describes his *puella* as an epic monster with as much hyperbole as he described his epic journey.[26] One of the effects of the grotesque image of Lesbia embracing three hundred adulterers at one time is to distance her from the human realities of separation and loss. She is no longer the beloved object of desire but an inhuman monster whom the speaker can mock and reject.

The speaker's message to Lesbia to "live and flourish with her adulterous lovers" at line 17 (*cum suis vivat valeatque moechis*) may be compared with Poem 5 and with the ideal of erotic bliss he evokes there. But here, unlike in Poem 5, living is associated with a destructive and corrupt way of being and is divorced completely from *amor* in the sense that Catullus defines it: a union involving both carnal and spiritual bonds. The fact that *vivat* is separated from *amor* puts Lesbia squarely in Caesar's impersonal world. Moreover, because Catullus equates *amor* and *vita* in Poem 5—with the suggestion that *vita* without *amor* is a kind of death—here Lesbia's loveless *vita* may also be regarded as a death. The image of Lesbia breaking the groins of her lovers (*omnium ilia rumpens*) as she holds them all at once (*simul*) in her embrace parallels all the risks (*omnia haec . . . temptare simul parati*) "Catullus" and his fellow-travelers might encounter in their adventuring out into the world. By objectifying her lovers and turning them all into an indistinguishable crowd of nobodies (*nullum amans vere*), Lesbia, like Caesar, turns all experience into vainglorious, impersonal *monimenta*. By suggesting a parallel between Lesbia's erotic degradation and Caesar's political conquests, Catullus implies that there is something morally repulsive about the imperialistic policies and ambitions of Rome.

The speaker's transformation of Lesbia into an object as awe inducing as one of Caesar's *monimenta*, however, depersonalizes her and thus shows that the speaker objectifies Lesbia much the same way as she dehumanizes her nameless lovers. The speaker's depiction of Lesbia, moreover, invokes male stereotypes about female sexuality. Lesbia comes to epitomize the image of the wayward woman—inherited from a tradition of invective against women—particularly with regard to their inability to restrain their sexual impulses. Thus, on the one hand, the speaker confirms his masculine identity by vilifying Lesbia, but on the other hand, he undermines that identity through his condemnation of a mode of conduct in which both Caesar and Lesbia are implicated. The speaker points up the monstrosity of female sexual excess, which defames women *and* suggests a link between the transgressions of Lesbia and those of Caesar. The speaker identifies himself with the activities and duties of respectable (male) Romans. Yet, through his retreat into poetic images and his devaluation of the excesses of conquest, he shows an alienation from male public culture.

Contradictory gender identities express the inherent ambivalence of the Catullan lover. One moment the speaker is a man crossing the Alps and reveling in the feats of mighty Caesar. The next moment he is a flower being crushed by the plow—a symbol of masculine power and mobility. Through his desire the lover is rendered both masculine and feminine, despite the figural castration of the speaker at the end of the poem. The poem concludes with the disturbing images of Lesbia as a cold, utilitarian plow and the speaker as a fragile flower. We know from Poem 5 that for Catullus, life and love are the same, so for the plow to annihilate the *flos*, which is the speaker's love, is to annihilate his *ego* altogether. Commentators of the poem have been nearly unanimous in regarding the poem's closing simile as final proof of Lesbia's ultimate and complete defeat of Catullus.[27] Moreover, on the whole, scholars have concurred that the simile unequivocally "transfers the mobile symbol of masculinity to Lesbia, while he himself (the speaker "Catullus") assumes the equally traditional sign of feminine sexuality."[28]

Ernst Fredricksmeyer comments on the symbolism of the plow and the flower.

> The collocation of the two images, of the flower for Catullus' love, and of the plough for Lesbia, is striking since both reverse traditional sexual symbolism. Elsewhere, Catullus himself used the flower as a picture for a virgin and even virginity itself, as a symbol for purity and delicate loveliness. And the plough, and ploughing, were well-known symbols for male sexual activity and, in particular, the phallus.[29]

In addition, the *flos* may recall a similar image of Sappho's in Fr. 105c. In Poem 51, Catullus identifies himself with Sappho by imitating her famous *phainetai moi* poem, and he also associates his beloved with Sappho by calling Clodia Lesbia. Here, through the flower image, Catullus maintains his association with Sappho and with the ideals she represents. But he excludes Lesbia from this association by not naming her and by identifying her with a male symbol, the plow, which destroys the flower. The flower image emphasizes, on the one hand, the chaste purity of the speaker's love and the sense of that love being removed from the world in a private, imagined space of pastoral innocence (*prati ultimi*). On the other hand, no matter how remote the meadow, the flower is ultimately vulnerable to the tangibly physical effects of the plow's destructive power. Although the loss of the virgin's innocence in the context of marriage destroys her sexual integrity and autonomy, it also leads to the productivity of the family. The utilitarian plow, however, has no place or productive use in a world whose only purpose is the appreciation of beauty.

Michael Putnam sees the whole process of the plow destroying the *flos* as a way for Catullus to show not only the emasculating effects of Lesbia on the speaker but also the conflict between the utilitarian civilizing forces of men and the innocence of the natural world.[30] The earlier epic expanse of places with its indications of imperialistic power is subsumed in the image of the inhuman plow destroying any living thing in its path. We can see the parallel here between Lesbia's brutality and Caesar's depersonalization of nature into *monimenta*. Putnam also points out that because plows are normally associated with *arva* and not *prata*, the interaction here of meadows and plows brings into collision the spheres of pastoral and georgic and shows that the seclusion of the imagined and ideal has no defense against the corruptions of the practical world.

That the plow enters the world of the *flos* accentuates the idea that the speaker's attempts to remove himself from the dehumanizing effects of civilization are unsuccessful and that his personal, erotic ideal cannot escape the corruption and degradation of an impersonal world. One touch of the plow destroys the *flos* completely. It is easy to see how Putnam and others have read the demise of the flower at the end of the poem as confirmation of the final devastation of the speaker's selfhood by Lesbia. Putnam clarifies this point: "It is Lesbia to whom all force is imputed at the poem's conclusion."[31] Despite the implications of the poem's closing simile, with its indications of violence and loss, the beauty of the image of the flower lying helpless in the field strips the moment of destruction of its gruesome reality. Like Virgil's famous simile in Book IX of the *Aeneid*,[32] in which the horror of Euryalus' death is transformed into a moment of beauty, here too we are uplifted beyond the ugliness of mechanized destruction to an image of beauty. While telling Lesbia (in his message) to look no longer at his love (*meum amorem*), the speaker then paradoxically produces a rather compelling and memorable visual image of that love. Catullus casts the conquests of both Caesar and Lesbia in a similar light of moral degradation as against his poetic rendering of the lover as a delicate, fragile flower that is victimized by the brutality of the world. We naturally turn our sympathies to that flower, whose innocence and beauty have immediate, sensual appeal (in contrast with the remote and abstract pleasures of foreign conquest and travel) as well as, and perhaps more importantly, moral superiority.

Catullus diverts attention from the grandiose attractions of the exterior world to the immediate and interior space of the realm of imagination. The whole poem shifts from the anonymity and multiplicity of the nameless crowd and distant peoples to the specificity of one flower. The pure, aesthetic beauty of Catullus' final image not only outstrips the images of destruction associated with Caesar and Lesbia but also affirms the voice of the poet whose power, paradoxically, contradicts the poem's implications of the lover's loss of selfhood.

Although it is true that Lesbia's force derives from the power of motion assigned to her in the image of the plow, her power is limited to a world in which utilitarian values and external motion are devalued by the poet. At the end of the poem, the speaker locates himself at the edge of the meadow — helpless in the face of an impersonal machine that seems to symbolize the dehumanizing effects of culture. By identifying himself with feminine sexuality and thus positioning himself more as a "woman" than as a "man," the speaker surrenders male power and privilege. Yet from his position at the edge of the meadow — that is, on the margins — the Catullan lover speaks with the authority of one with the prerogative of seeing *and* proscribing how he and Lesbia will be seen by others. The speaker's use of the subjunctive in lines 17 and 21 (*vivat, nec respectet,* "Let her live," "Let her not look") conveys a sense of authority which belies the speaker's presentation of himself as a flower powerless to defend itself against outside forces.

Indeed, the male lover, with his magisterial rhetoric, does not "let his mistress look" at his love. Rather, she becomes an object of *his* looking.[33] He imagined himself earlier "viewing the memorials of mighty Caesar," and now he gazes at the imagined spectacle of his mistress mightily embracing three hundred men at once. Further, in the last few lines of the poem, the speaker directs our gaze toward himself (*meum amorem*) and away from the woman who may not look. Although he does not want Lesbia to look at his love, he appears to want his audience to turn its attention to the image of the flower, which symbolizes his love. The grand geographical sweep in the opening catalogue and the rapacious mobility of world travel and conquest narrow down in time and space to the isolated, immobile flower. The action of the passing plow "touching" a flower at the edge of the meadow occurs in a kind of slow motion compared with the activities of traversing vast distances and breaking (*rumpens*) the groins of three hundred men at one time.

By lingering on the image of one flower and focusing on its demise as a consequence of a *culpa,* the speaker evokes sympathy for a kind of love previously untouched by the moral degeneracy associated with conquest, the indifferent mowing down of nameless living things. Although the concluding image of the poem seems to emphasize destruction and loss, the speaker turns our attention not only to the cruel and indifferent plow but also to the pristine beauty of a singular nameless and remote flower. I would thus argue that the image of the *flos* freezes all motion and shows, through its power to captivate, the far greater appeal of the poet's inward journey — to a place at the edge of the meadow from which we are able to see most clearly the excesses of culture. The plow merely passes by (*praetereunte*), but it is the flower's beauty and the pathos of its destruction which, at the end, the speaker summons us to see and to remember.

CHAPTER THREE

Elegiac Woman
Fantasy, *Materia*, and Male Desire in Propertius' *Monobiblos*

OF THE ELEGIAC POETS, Propertius is considered by many to be the inventor of the image of the *servitium amoris*.[1] The Propertian lover appears to demonstrate *par excellence* the elegiac *topos* of the male narrator as enslaved and the female narrative subject as his enslaver. As I will argue in this chapter, however, despite Propertius' realist narrative strategies, particularly in Book 1, the elegiac woman is not portrayed primarily as a beloved but rather as narrative *materia* in the poet's literary discourse. In two recent essays on deciphering the "real" existences of elegiac mistresses,[2] Maria Wyke offers a compelling argument that "Cynthia is depicted as matter for poetic composition, not as a woman to be wooed through writing." Wyke applies her argument mainly to Books 2–4 and maintains that Book 1 stresses the portrayal of Cynthia as a flesh and blood woman who does not become intimately associated with the practice of writing until Book 2. I will argue, however, that even in Book 1, despite her apparent dramatic presence, Cynthia is depicted primarily as a "woman in a text"—a text that inscribes male desire and also reflects the self-conscious literary concerns of the poet. My analyses of Propertius' amatory texts will take into account what has, for the most part, been ignored: the gender specificity of Propertius' portrayals of Cynthia and of the ways desire is constituted in his poems.

Because of their emphasis on devices of realism, the poems in the *Monobiblos* provide fruitful opportunities for an examination of Propertius' depiction of Cynthia as beloved and as narrative *materia*. Through an analysis of four poems from the *Monobiblos*, I will show that Propertius presents his elegiac mistress as a pictorial *object* that arouses the lover's erotic fantasies *and* serves as a vehicle for his artistic fame. Even though Propertius represents Cynthia as both *dura* (strong) and *docta* (learned), the male narrator in Book 1 often imagines his mistress either in an ideal state of captivity and helplessness, or he identifies her exclusively with a nonrational nature. Further, I will argue that even in poems that emphasize most clearly the *amator*'s subservience toward Cynthia, as in the opening elegy, Propertius nonetheless portrays her as little more than a vehicle for his artistic fame and a function of his literary discourse. Despite the appearance of a more or less egalitarian union between men and women in Propertian elegy (e.g., Georg Luck asserted that elegists "honestly believed in the equality of women"),[3] I believe that an examination of poems in the first book shows that amatory relations in Propertius' elegies are closely bound up with the "realities" of male domination and power. Cynthia is often depicted either as a helpless victim who needs the guardianship of her male lover *or* as a creature of uncontrolled passion and emotion—a potentially dangerous source of disorder.

Elegy 1.1

Because of its programmatic nature and its apparent reliance on devices of realism, Propertius' first elegy in the *Monobiblos* is a good place to begin our discussion of his portrayal of Cynthia as a woman in a text and to examine how male desire is inscribed in poems that appear to emphasize the speaker's helplessness and passivity.

>   Cynthia prima suis miserum me cepit ocellis,
>   contactum nullis ante cupidinibus.
>   tum mihi constantis deiecit lumina fastus
>   et caput impositis pressit Amor pedibus,
> 5   donec me docuit castas odisse puellas
>   improbus, et nullo vivere consilio.
>   et mihi iam toto furor hic non deficit anno,
>   cum tamen adversos cogor habere deos.
>   Milanion nullos fugiendo, Tulle, labores
> 10   saevitiam durae contudit Iasidos.
>   nam modo Partheniis amens errabat in antris,
>   ibat et hirsutas ille videre feras;

      ille etiam Hylaei percussus vulnere rami
         saucius Arcadiis rupibus ingemuit.
15 ergo velocem potuit domuisse puellam:
         tantum in amore preces et bene facta valent.
      in me tardus Amor non ullas cogitat artis,
         nec meminit notas, ut prius, ire vias.
      at vos, deductae quibus est fallacia lunae
20   et labor in magicis sacra piare focis,
      en agedum dominae mentem convertite nostrae,
         et facite illa meo palleat ore magis!
      tunc ego crediderim vobis et sidera et amnis
         posse Cytinaeis ducere carminibus.
25 et vos, qui sero lapsum revocatis, amici,
         quaerite non sani pectoris auxilia.
      fortiter et ferrum saevos patiemur et ignis,
         sit modo libertas quae velit ira loqui.
      ferte per extremas gentis et ferte per undas,
30   qua non ulla meum femina norit iter.
      vos remanete, quibus facili deus annuit aure,
         sitis et in tuto semper amore pares.
      in me nostra Venus noctes exercet amaras,
         et nullo vacuus tempore defit Amor.
35 hoc, moneo, vitate malum: sua quemque moretur
         cura, neque assueto mutet amore locum.
      quod si quis monitis tardas adverterit auris,
         heu referet quanto verba dolore mea!

[First Cynthia made me, to my unhappiness, her prisoner with her lovely eyes, me, who had been touched by no desires before. Then Amor forced down my eyes, that had shown a firm pride, and pressed my head beneath his feet, until he taught me to hate chaste women, that shameless one, and to live without a guiding principle. And my frenzy already has lasted incessantly for a whole year, but nevertheless I must have the gods against me. I am addressing myself to you, Tullus. By shunning no toils whatsoever, Milanion crumbled the savage resistance of Iasus' haughty daughter. For at times he used to roam about the Parthenian glens in a state of frenzy, at times he also went repeatedly to face shaggy beasts. That hero was even hurt by a blow from Hylaeus' club, and wounded, broke into moaning on Arcadian rocks. Thus he was able to tame and win the swift-footed girl; such is the power of prayers and good actions in love. In my case, however, Amor is tardy and does not devise any crafts, and he no longer remembers to travel well-known roads, as before. But you, who scheme to pull down the moon and labor to perform appeasing sacrifices on magic hearths, look, go ahead, convert the mind of our mistress and make her face paler than mine! Then I would be ready to believe you that you are able to pull the stars and streams by the magic chants of the sorceress from Cytaea. And you, my friends, who call me back too late, after I have fallen, look for remedies for an unsound heart! Bravely we will endure the sword and the savage fire if only freedom be granted to say what my anger wishes! Carry me across the nations at the end of the world and across the sea, where no woman knows where I am! You stay behind, to whom the god inclines a gracious ear, and I wish that you be equal partners in a secure love. In my case Venus plies bitter nights against me, and at no time does Love either rest or cease. Avoid this evil, I warn you. May each be detained by his own dear worry, and may he not stray from his familiar love. But if anyone heeds my warning too late, alas, how painfully he will recall, my words!]

No one could deny that on the face of it, the speaker introduces himself to us as wretchedly unhappy (*miserum me*). From the beginning, he characterizes himself as being subject to an agency outside himself, captive of an external force. Cynthia, on the other hand, is an active agent who has ensnared (*cepit*) the speaker with her eyes. Moreover, the opening words of the poem, *"Cynthia prima,"* imply that Cynthia will be the subject of the poem and the focus of the speaker's attention. Yet we soon discover that what really concerns the speaker is his own role as poet. Cynthia herself is not mentioned again in the poem; she is merely a function of the poet-lover's self-conscious awareness of his literary commitments and of his place in literary tradition.

In spite of the speaker's putative misery, he seems to convey a sense of delight in his own state of captivity. The use of the diminutive form in *ocellis* (line 1) communicates affectionate play and lightheartedness rather than the heaviness we might expect to be associated with the speaker's imprisoned condition. The speaker describes the process of becoming enslaved by love in tangibly physical terms: he had been touched (*contactum,* line 2) by no desires before, and *Amor* forced the speaker's eyes down and pressed the speaker's head (*caput,* line 4) beneath *Amor*'s feet (*pedibus,* line 4). Although it is a *topos* in the tradition of love poetry to describe the effects of *eros* in physical terms,[4] Propertius' physical descriptions here depart in an important way from those of his predecessors. Both Sappho and Catullus use physical detail to describe an emotional and physical loss of control which closely associates erotic experience with death or loss of identity.[5] In contrast, Propertius describes the speaker's enslavement to love, not as an internal emotional event, but as an external action that takes place in the world of military conquest.

Propertius' military metaphor to describe the experience of falling in love highlights the way in which private and public discourses are deeply interwoven. The language of the elegiac lover is presented as part of a public discourse. By depicting his lover as a fighter on the battlefield (even a defeated one), Propertius portrays a lover whose poetry and practices are bound up inextricably in the masculine sphere of public achievement. Even though Propertius' use of military imagery in an amatory context is, to be sure, a display of literary ingenuity, it nonetheless draws on the association of Love and War which is persistent in both the Greek and Roman traditions. The Trojan War is the primary example of this association; it is implicit in the story told of Aphrodite and Ares in the *Odyssey* and is explicit in the speech of Phaedrus in Plato's *Symposium*.[6] Moreover, in the invocation to Venus at the start of *De Rerum Natura*, Lucretius makes clear that Venus' powers of nurture and inspiration are fruitless without her association with Mars, whose disruptive and destructive influence must be tamed constantly by Venus. Love and peace cannot flourish unless Venus maintains her vanquishing hold on Mars. Thus Lucretius suggests, paradoxically, that love—symbolized by Venus—can only bring peace to mortals if the lover learns to conquer and enslave the beloved. *Amor*'s defeat of the narrator in Propertius' poem reiterates a traditional paradigm for amatory relations in which conquest and subjugation of the other are viewed as integral to amatory experience. In addition, that the language of warfare becomes the language of love suggests the intertwining of the seemingly "private" discourse of the lover and the public discourse of martial valor.

Indeed, Propertius portrays *Amor* much like a Roman general defeating his enemies. However, the action of *Amor* trampling the speaker's head with his feet reverses the traditional gesture of victory in battle, in which the victor places his foot on the chest of his victim before despoiling him.[7] Here, the victim rather than the victor is the one who records the event. The speaker thus seems to be far more in control than his "wretchedness" would imply. In his analysis of the poem, Hans-Peter Stahl assumes that the point of view offered here of the victim with his head under the feet of his conqueror necessarily implies that pain and torture are the results of this action.[8] But the incongruity in Propertius' mock-heroic image of *Amor*'s defeat of the lover seems more humorous than tragic.

Unlike the Catullan lover, the speaker does not, with one part of himself, reject his "shameless" erotic feelings, nor does he attempt to overcome them. In fact, the speaker makes it clear that his new imprudent way of living (*nullo vivere consilio*) is taught to him by a god. Not only does this remove any agency from the speaker himself but it also, paradoxically, makes it seem as though the speaker is improving himself by learning an important lesson from his mentor. In addition, the speaker describes himself moving from one extreme to the other, from an attitude of absolute aversion to sexuality to an absolute dedication to it, signified by his hatred of chaste women. The fact that the speaker describes his desire as a form of hate reveals the violence of his emotions yet also ostensibly expresses the Catullan conflict in which erotic impulses are necessarily characterized by an ambivalent mixture of love and hate. Critics have generally understood the speaker's abrupt change from chastity to sexuality as a way for Propertius to show how the speaker is taken by love against his will. But they fail to see the playfulness in the hyperbolic way the speaker describes his position. Not only is he converted to sexuality but he also learns to "hate chaste girls." Not only is the speaker *not* scandalized by his hatred of chaste girls but, on the contrary, he seems to relish his new role.

Further, the dispassionate tone in the speaker's declaration belies any sense of conflict or suffering. Embedded in Propertius' erotic discourse is an awareness of audience expectations as to the role of the lover and his particular mode of expression. The fact that the lover speaks about his amatory situation in the past tense suggests that he is at a remove from his feelings and also shows that he is departing in an important way from the Catullan tradition, which envisions the lover as hopelessly bound in a present tense of conflict and introspective self-analysis. The real thrust of Propertius' erotic discourse here is directed neither toward himself nor toward his beloved but rather toward his audience and the particular benefit it can derive from his experience. As Poem 1 progresses, the speaker's purpose in telling his story becomes clearer: to explain, illustrate, and instruct from the *exemplum* of his personal experience. That the speaker describes his situation in quasi-mythological terms, as fighting and losing a battle with a mythological figure, stresses the more mythical, abstract, and universal aspects of his amatory struggles. Both he and his mistress become mythical figures in a story that the lover hopes will bring him *fama*.

The mythological *exemplum* of Milanion and Atalanta reinforces Propertius' presentation of the poet-lover as a teacher who has important truths to pass on to his community. His apostrophe to Tullus at line 9, at the moment when he embarks on his mythological tale, accentuates Propertius' instructive tone by heightening our awareness that the speaker is telling this story for the benefit of others. Whether one knows who the actual Tullus was or not, the realism and specificity in the mention of his name bring into focus the world outside the poem. The *amator*'s self-conscious awareness of the presence of an audience shows that he is telling the story not merely to highlight aspects of his own personal situation (either for himself or for others) but to express messages that have more universal application.

One of the messages implicit in Propertius' version of the story of Milanion and Atalanta is in the way the figure of Milanion embodies the values of both the hero and the lover. Milanion's *exemplum* reinforces, in a more serious vein, Propertius' earlier image of the lover as a soldier and its associations with heroic values. Propertius contradicts the stereotypical association of effeminacy and inaction with the lover.[9] Instead, he presents an example that shows the lover in a heroic context in which he courageously endures the pain of *amor* and fearlessly encounters all obstacles, which not only wins glory for the hero but captures the object of desire as well. Even though Milanion is not a soldier, he is a fighter who exhibits traditional heroic qualities (risking body and soul for what one desires). The implied parallel between Milanion and Atalanta and the speaker and his mistress suggests a paradigm for amatory relations in which the male lover "overtakes" the reluctant female—a paradigm that implies the inevitability of male dominance over women. Indeed, in lines 10 and 15, the words Propertius uses to describe Milanion's success with Atalanta—*contudit* and *domuisse*—suggest that Propertius' ideal lover wins his mistress not by wooing her but by "crushing" or "subduing" her. The violence implicit in *contundere* reiterates *Amor*'s earlier violence toward the *amator* himself. But in the mythological *exemplum*, the speaker imagines the lover in the position of *Amor* and the woman in the role of the speaker. Like the speaker, Atalanta too surrenders to *Amor* and gives up her stubborn pride. The correlation between the speaker and Milanion thus suggests that the speaker imagines himself in the role of subduer rather than captive and in turn pictures the woman as *his* captive. Perhaps the *amator*'s delight in his own captivity bespeaks an awareness that the positions of captor and captive become, in matters of love, like those in war, often reversed.

Although the speaker's mythological *exemplum* ennobles the pursuit of love and demonstrates the eventual rewards that can come to the suffering lover, the myth also offers an extreme contrast to the speaker's own situation. Atalanta shows that even the most chaste, resistant girls can give in to love. But clearly, because Cynthia remains "chaste" (as far as the *amator* is concerned), the speaker's situation does not fit the norm established by the myth. On the one hand, this serves to heighten the speaker's suffering, but on the other hand, it demonstrates that his love for Cynthia goes far beyond normal expectations. The myth suggests that the speaker's job is more difficult than Milanion's and that his persistence and devotion are greater. The speaker's self-effacing declaration, *in me tardus Amor non ullas cogitat artis*, is usually taken to reinforce the uniqueness of the speaker's love by emphasizing his failure compared with Milanion's success. Even though the speaker admits that in his case, *Amor* has not devised any crafts to help him, we have just seen ample evidence of the speaker's wit and poetic craft in his conceit of the lover as both soldier and hero.

The speaker's sudden entreaty for help from sorceresses at lines 20–22 seems to reinforce his presentation of himself as desperate and powerless.[10] On the surface, the speaker's apostrophe to witches can be read as a new way for him to express the hopelessness of his amatory situation. But here Propertius' evocation of erotic magic draws on the trope of witches, which has a long tradition in Greek and Roman literature, particularly in myths concerning courtship and marriage.[11] This tradition can be seen most notably in the figures of Circe, Deianeira, and Medea. The theme of love magic can also be traced in Apollonius' depiction of Medea in Book 4 of the *Argonautica*, Theocritus' story of erotic magic in his second idyll, and Virgil's adaptation of Theocritus' poem in his eighth eclogue. What seems remarkable about Propertius' discourse on erotic magic is the way traditional gender positions are reversed. In Propertius' poem, a male narrator calls on female witches to "convert" the mind of his mistress even though witches typically use their magic to attract males or take revenge on them if the males do not reciprocate. Moreover, the speaker's invocation to those whose practice it is to draw the moon down from the sky (19) specifically echoes the voice of the sorceress in Virgil's Eclogue 8 as she expresses her belief that "songs can even draw the moon from the sky" (*carmina vel caelo possunt deducere lunam*, line 69). In addition, the allusion to Medea in line 24[12] reinforces the implications of female sorcery in the speaker's invocation (*at vos*). The erotic magic of Medea, like that of Circe, Deianeira, and Theocritus' witch Simaetha, emphasizes not only the theme of unmitigated desire but also the potential transformation of love magic into black magic. As Faraone argues, erotic magical rituals aimed at attracting men seem to be concerned primarily with "enervating and thereby controlling the 'normally' active male, while those magic rituals aimed at women have a completely different orientation, their primary goal being to rouse up and energize the 'naturally' passive female."[13] The object of the narrator's plea to "change the mind" of his mistress by no means seems to be to stimulate desire in her or to "energize" her. Rather, Propertius' *amator* asks that Cynthia's cheek be made as pale as his is (*et facite illa meo palleat ore magis!*). The erotic magic that the speaker invokes here seeks to debilitate and control the mistress rather than to arouse her. Moreover, the implications of black magic—with its deadly consequences for the recalcitrant object of desire—suggest motives of revenge on the part of the speaker and a desire to undermine the woman's position as *domina*.

But there is humor in the speaker's evocation of magic as well. In his apostrophes both to witches and to friends, the speaker chooses ludicrously impossible remedies that he clearly considers neither credible nor potent. At line 25 the speaker himself says that he is beyond remedies: *et vos, qui sero lapsum revocatis, amici.* How can his friends possibly help him when, by his own admission, they are already too late? He asks witches and friends to do the impossible: to pull down the moon and the stars and to exorcise the love from his heart either by the knife or by fire. Presenting two impossible alternatives functions as a rhetorical gesture to heighten the speaker's desperate situation. But the hyperbolic images of being carried to the end of the earth where there are no women and enduring the sword and fire (*fortiter et ferrum saevos patiemur et ignis / sit modo libertas quae velit ira loqui. / ferte per extremas gentis et ferte per undas, / qua non ulla meum femina norit iter*) take the speaker's emotional situation to ludicrously literal extremes. We can detect perhaps more than a hint of mockery of the lover's excesses here. Asking the sorceresses to make Cynthia even paler than he is, in the middle of his emotional entreaty, reveals a concern for concrete detail which evokes comedy instead of tragedy and suggests mockery of the clichés of romantic expression. Stahl, on the other hand, sees no humor in the speaker's description of his emotional "desperation." "The poetical surprise of lines 18–30 lies in the fact that Propertius has found a still wider range of expression of his personal isolation: after Cynthia, Amor, the gods, Milanion, Tullus, now even witches (a traditional help in an irrational situation) and volunteering friends are introduced and prove to be of no avail; whereas the group of 'the others' receives accretion, the outline of his loneliness becomes still sharper: *definitio e contrario*."[14] The speaker himself undercuts his desperate emotional stance by announcing at line 28 that his amatory suffering is tied to an aesthetic purpose. Saying that he would endure any amount of suffering if only he has the freedom to express his feelings suggests that literary expression is the antidote to the lover's pain and, more importantly, counterbalances the image of the enslavement of the lover with that of the freedom of the poet.

The speaker's desperate apostrophes, rather than reinforcing a presentation of a truly helpless self, expose the literary strategy at work here, in which the speaker's unique erotic situation becomes a new *exemplum* to be used by succeeding generations of lovers. In the last eight lines of the poem the speaker reveals his self-conscious awareness of his place in the literary tradition of love poetry. Stahl reads the speaker's final apostrophe to the lovers he leaves behind as his "final statement of his now utter separation and isolation."[15] It is true that the speaker separates himself from the world of happy lovers, but in so doing he creates out of his entirely unique situation a new *exemplum* with its own message. Stahl reads the *vos* at line 31 as a contrast to rather than a continuation of *at vos* at line 19. I would argue, however, that *vos* at line 31 does continue a pattern in which the speaker demonstrates or claims that his particular fate is so unique as to find no parallel anywhere, even in myth.

At the beginning of line 33, the speaker again emphasizes the uniqueness of his position (*in me*). The threefold repetition of *vos* and the repetition of *in me* here accentuate the singularity of his erotic situation. But despite the speaker's emphasis on his personal dilemma, *nostra* attached to Venus links the speaker to the wider concerns of all lovers. Although the speaker describes his situation as hopeless, with nights of torment and unceasing, lonely *amor*, the very singularity of that experience becomes an *exemplum* of *hoc malum*. From this example the speaker draws out a message of warning (lines 35 and 36), a message that establishes another norm for *amor* which has a lesson in it for all lovers to come.

The speaker's final emphasis is not on his tormented emotional state but on his message derived from the *exemplum* artfully constructed from painful erotic experience. The pain shifts from that of the speaker to that of lovers who do not heed his warning (*heu referet quanto verba dolore mea*). The speaker himself is associated not with his erotic torment and his helplessness at the end but with his words (*mea verba*). Before, it was *Amor* who was slow (*tardus Amor*) to help; now it is the ears of other lovers who are slow (*tardas auris*) to listen. Now the speaker rather than *Amor* teaches a lesson. In the end, the lover is assimilated to the poet, who has transformed the torture of love into the artifice of *exemplum*. Despite the speaker's claim in the first line of the poem that Cynthia is *his* captor, we see that this is little more than a rhetorical gesture to establish his particular aesthetic stance as a writer of elegies. The speaker, as love poet, is very much in control. Indeed, his warning at the end is spoken with an oracular authority (his use of the imperative in *vitate malum* and hortatory subjunctives *moretur, mutet* in lines 35 and 36) that belies his protestations of subservience toward his mistress. The air of authority expressed here not only undermines the speaker's avowed position as *servus amoris* but also assumes, on the part of the speaker, a privileged relation to language, the traditionally masculine prerogative to name and write his desire.[16] Indeed, the first poem in the *Monobiblos* establishes a position for

Elegiac Woman

the male lover in which his "captivity" is a fiction within a narrative he both defines and describes. The woman, as we will see clearly in 1.7, 1.3, and 1.11, is a function of the narrator's text—*his* story.

Elegy 1.7

Addressing the epic poet Ponticus, the speaker in Poem 1.7 explicitly rejects the values associated with martial conquest and the heroic ethos generally expressed in epic poetry. In the context of asserting his elegiac values against those in the epic tradition, the speaker substitutes Cynthia as his preferred subject for his literary productions. To show Ponticus that the lover's *materia* for his writing is not only worthy but indeed superior to that in epic, he describes it (Cynthia) as being both *dura* and *docta*. But while scorning these heroic values the speaker nonetheless reconfigures the heroic ethos in a way that allows him to play the epic hero and thus occupy the subject position of the heroic male.[17] That subject position, I shall argue, gives rise to stereotypically masculine binary views of the mistress as either an adversary to overcome (*dura*) or an audience (*docta*) to impress with literary prowess.

      Dum tibi Cadmeae dicuntur, Pontice, Thebae
          armaque fraternae tristia militiae,
      atque, ita sim felix, primo contendis Homero,
          (sint modo fata tuis mollia carminibus:)
5   nos, ut consuemus, nostros agitamus amores,
          atque aliquid duram quaerimus in dominam;
      nec tantum ingenio quantum servire dolori
          cogor et aetatis tempora dura queri.
      hic mihi conteritur vitae modus, haec mea fama est,
10   hinc cupio nomen carminis ire mei.
      me laudent doctae solum placuisse puellae,
          Pontice, et iniustas saepe tulisse minas;
      me legat assidue post haec neglectus amator,
          et prosint illi cognita nostra mala.
15   te quoque si certo puer hic concusserit arcu
          (quod nolim nostros, heu, voluisse deos),
      longe castra tibi, longe miser agmina septem
          flebis in aeterno surda iacere situ;
      et frustra cupies mollem componere versum,
20   nec tibi subiciet carmina serus amor.
      tum me non humilem mirabere saepe poetam,

>   tunc ego Romanis praeferar ingeniis;
>   nec poterunt iuvenes nostro reticere sepulcro
>   'Ardoris nostri magne poeta, iaces.'
> 25 tu cave nostra tuo contemnas carmina fastu:
>   saepe venit magno faenore tardus amor.

[While you, Ponticus, sing of Cadmean Thebes, and the grievous arms of fraternal battle, and—as I wish to be happy—you contend with Homer the master, may the Fates be kind to your songs, we are, as we are accustomed, doing our love poems, and seeking some means to soften our harsh mistress; I am forced to serve not so much my talent as my pain, and to grieve over the harsh times of my youth. This is the life that wears me down, this is my fame, and hence comes the glory I seek from my songs: Let my praise be that I alone pleased a talented girl, Ponticus, and often bore her unjust threats. Let the despised lover hereafter read me, and may the study of our sorrows help him. If you, too, are shaken by the boy's unfailing arrow (I do not wish our gods to have decreed this for you), then, unhappy man, you will realize amid tears that for you the camp is far away, the seven armies far away, lying in silence, buried in the eternal rust of oblivion. And in vain you will long to compose delicate verse, nor will belated Love supply you with songs. Then you will often admire me as no lowly poet, then I will be preferred among Roman literary talents. The youths will not keep silence by my grave: "Here you lie," they will say, "the great poet of our ardor." Take care your pride does not despise our songs: Late Love often comes exacting a heavy interest.]

The elegy opens with the speaker's contrast between his own poetic concerns and those of Ponticus: Ponticus writes epics whose subject is war and fraternal dissent, but the speaker is occupied with his "humble" poems about love. Where Ponticus has chosen the lofty goal of contending with Homer, the love poet merely wants to find something (*aliquid*) that will soften his harsh mistress (*duram dominam*). The position of the elegist in relation to the epic poet is clear. He adopts the appropriate attitude of deference toward the art that was traditionally regarded as the only adequate way to express the greatness in man. The literary and social prestige of the epic poet were unquestionable. The speaker gives the appearance of paying homage to epic poetry by imitating its grand style at the beginning. Yet the speaker's praise of Ponticus and his style is tinged with irony and ambiguity. First, the exaggerated quality of the speaker's admiration calls his sincerity into question. Second, the speaker's parenthetical hope that the songs of Ponticus will not be forgotten (*sint modo fata tuis mollia carminibus*) injects an ominous note into an atmosphere of grandiose aspirations and implies that perhaps the *fata* will be harsh rather than merciful to those songs.

Although the speaker claims to embrace a way of life opposite that of Ponticus ("While you . . . *I*"), the language with which he explains that life suggests that it is merely another version of the traditional heroic ethos. The speaker insists that he, compared with the epic poets, is preoccupied with pursuing his desires and seeking some way to soften his harsh mistress. The antiheroic passivity expected of an elegiac poet, however, is undercut by the speaker's use of *agitamus* in line 5 to describe the activity typical of love poets. Indeed, the sense of motion and the possible implications of pursuing and hunting in *agitamus* suggest a level of manly exertion consistent with traditional heroic values. Further, the actions of pursuing an object single-mindedly and attempting to overcome a difficult adversary (in the lover's case, his *duram dominam* in place of other male fighters) reiterate rather than contradict the combat mentality of heroic males. Cynthia is deserving of the speaker's attention *and* his pursuit precisely because her hardheartedness makes her a worthy enough opponent. In other words, the narrator's representation of Cynthia as *dura* creates the impetus for him to activate and articulate *his* desires.

In fact, right after the speaker mentions his harsh *domina,* we learn that it is not really her whom he serves but rather his own talent. Although he claims to be serving his pain and not his *ingenium* (lines 7 and 8), he immediately associates his painful way of life as a lover with his fame as a poet: *hic mihi conteritur vitae modus, haec mea fama est.* The syntactical link between his *vitae modus* (as the suffering lover) and his *fama* shows that the lover's pain is closely bound up with winning immortality for himself as a poet. The repetition of personal pronouns at line 9 (*mihi, mea*) emphasizes the speaker's pride in asserting his *vitae modus* against that of Ponticus and that expressed in the epic tradition. The speaker's triumphant tone here, which contradicts his earlier stance of humility, reinforces his ironic attitude toward the triviality of *his* achievements and the grandiosity of those of Ponticus.

At line 10, desire (*cupio*) is linked not to the *puella* but to the glory of the speaker's songs. The main concern of the speaker is for the praise he will receive because of his liaison with a *docta puella*. Indeed, the praise he seeks is dependent on his ability to be the only one who can please (*solum placuisse*) not just any *puella* but one who is *docta*. As before when he imagined Cynthia as an obstacle worthy of his erotic prowess, here he alludes to her talent not so much in terms of its worth in its own right but in terms of the way it may reflect on him and thus win him more praise.

That the speaker is obsessed with his own talents—indeed his own oracular abilities—is evident in the magisterial way he speaks to Ponticus in the rest of the poem. Not only does this tone contradict his claims of passive subservience, it also reiterates the attitudes of militancy and competition which are traditionally disavowed by the elegiac poet. In the previous elegy, 1.6, the speaker clearly rejects the *ethos* of the public life: *non ego sum laudi, non natus idoneus armis: / hanc me militiam fata subire volunt* [I was born unfit for glory, unfit for arms, this is the warfare the Fates would have me bear] (lines 29 and 30). But in 1.7 we see that it is not only glory the speaker is after (and believes he will receive) but that he wants to assert his superior talent in a hierarchy of men of genius: *tum me non humilem mirabere saepe poetam, / tunc ego Romanis praeferar ingeniis* [Then you will often admire me as no insignificant poet, and I will be preferred among Rome's men of genius] (lines 21 and 22). Such an assertion hardly constitutes the antiheroic passivity expected of the elegiac lover. On the contrary, it merely reconfigures the heroic, martial ethos in a way that perpetuates the aggressive, adversarial modes of conduct and discourse typical of heroes on the battlefield. In fact, the speaker's taunting of Ponticus and his confident assertions that he will ultimately "win" in the battle of the *ingenia* sound very similar to Achilles or Aeneas deriding their opponents before killing them.

As the speaker warns at line 15, if the epic poet should suddenly be struck by love he would not have the vocabulary at his disposal, the aesthetic resources to "compose" himself. Moreover, the use of *cupio* at line 19 (*et frustra cupies mollem componere versum*) in relation to Ponticus is associated not with the union between the lover and his beloved but with the ability to compose (*componere*). In the last half of the poem, the speaker's use of the future tense for what will happen to Ponticus points to the inevitability of the power of love over human beings. In addition, the hypnotic effect of repeating again and again what, in fact, *will* happen displays a magisterial power that elevates the love poet to prophetic status. The speaker's earlier statement that he serves his pain rather than his talent was a rhetorical gesture of humility, one that enabled him to establish his position as a writer of love poems rather than a writer of epics. And the speaker's emotional servitude is the vehicle through which he comes to be remembered as a great poet and to defeat his literary rivals in securing a place for himself in posterity.

Ironically, the epic poet who scorns the lover's art and the state of servitude implied in the position of the lover will end up, according to the speaker, being a slave to his emotions, devoid of the emotional or literary resources to heal himself. Another irony is that the speaker, the writer of elegies, is the one who is entirely "composed" and has glory in the area where men are the most vulnerable and powerless. In lines 17–20 the speaker implies that emotional composure and the composing of poems are the same; the answer to poor Ponticus' emotionally helpless state is the *componere* of *mollem versum*, not the appearance of the beloved. Moreover, the speaker asserts that it will be the elegiac poet who shall be a hero to young men in love. He reconstructs himself as a heroic paradigm in the manner of epic heroes—whose exploits and attributes he argues are of no use where personal existence is at stake.

In the last line of the poem, the speaker consolidates his appropriation of male public culture by using the language of the commercial world to assert his dominance in that culture: *saepe venit magno faenore tardus amor* [Late love often comes exacting a heavy interest]. The speaker not only makes his point in a language Ponticus can understand but also demonstrates the way in which the power of *amor* extends into the realm of practical affairs. By mingling the discourses of love and money, the speaker shows that he can have power in the world of Ponticus. The speaker's triumphant announcement of his supremacy in the world of Roman literary talents suggests that the elegiac stance of servitude toward the mistress is nothing more than a ruse to create an alternative heroic ethos for the male protagonist. We shall see in the following discussion of *Elegies* 1.3 and 1.11 how the lover's fantasies of control over a helpless and captive mistress are played out to ensure his fame and to perpetuate a status that reinforces masculine prerogative and privilege.

Elegy 1.3

Recent work in feminist psychoanalytic theory provides a framework for interpreting the tension in 1.3 between the real and ideal Cynthias. In their provocative works, Luce Irigaray ("This Sex Which Is Not One") and Jessica Benjamin (*The Bonds of Love*) critique Freud's accounts of both male and female desire and sexuality.[18] In particular, Irigaray unravels Freudian theory about the *gaze* as a phallic activity linked to a desire for mastery of the object (the woman).[19] Irigaray and Benjamin challenge the idea—one they regard as dominant in the Western tradition—that the woman is a mirror for male desire ("penis envy") and that woman's object status, her lack of an active desire of her own, and her passivity are all hallmarks of the feminine. In her interpretation of Freudian theory, Irigaray demonstrates how the gaze is crucial in securing the domination of the male. Her argument that women are turned into statues in the process of specularization—through the agency of the look that sees only a reflection of the observer's own desires—seems especially useful in reading both 1.3 and 1.11. I will argue that in both poems Propertius' narrator turns his mistress into an object to gaze at and that this encounter with an *objectified other* gives rise to the image of the woman as either a dangerous siren or an unruly hag who is a potential threat to the narrator's position of domination.

Maria Wyke agrees that despite the apparent reversal of sex roles in Propertius' elegiac texts, those texts do not depict female power, nor do they elaborate a role for the female subject which grants her an elevated social status.

> The heterodoxy of the elegiac portrayal of love, therefore, lies in the absence of a political or social role for the male narrator, not in any attempt to provide or demand a political role for the female subject. The temporary alignment with a sexually unrestrained mistress whom Augustan elegy depicts does not bestow on the female a new, challenging role but alienates the male from his traditional responsibilities. The elegiac poets exploit the traditional methods of ordering female sexuality which locate the sexually unrestrained and therefore socially ineffective female on the margins of society in order to portray their first-person heroes as displaced from a central position in the social categories of Augustan Rome.[20]

Wyke is right in pointing out that elegiac texts are "more generally concerned with male servitude, not female mastery."[21] But her argument centers on refuting the view that elegiac poets are interested in empowering women and raising their social status through an unconventional portrayal of gender relations. Wyke does not, however, consider the full implications of the elegiac lover's identification of his mistress with her *function* in literary discourse — as *materia* for poetic production. *Elegies* 1.3 and 1.11 both demonstrate that the subordination of the woman as beloved to the woman as *materia* reveals a version of male desire which devalues women and turns them into objects in male fantasies of erotic domination.

Propertius 1.3 has prompted a number of important and influential studies.[22] Although scholars have emphasized somewhat different critical approaches to the poem, the focus has been the tension between the reality and the idealization of the lover and his mistress. R. O. A. M. Lyne tells us that 1.3 "is about Cynthia the woman of wonder, the idealised creation of Propertius' own mind, and Cynthia the woman of reality who inevitably reveals herself, and breaks in upon the eggshell world of dreams."[23] Likewise, Daniel Harmon argues that "1.3 portrays an occasion upon which the poet envisions an encounter with Cynthia while exploring reality through fantasy."[24] Leo Curran's study emphasizes "the contrast between the epic world with its serene and accessible heroines and the real world of capricious and hot-tempered mistresses."[25] These scholars offer many illuminating insights about the poem, but their readings tend to privilege and romanticize the male perspective of the narrator. More important is their failure to question male assumptions about desire or to consider the gender-specific nature of desire which the poem expresses. In my analysis, I will explore how a version of male desire is constituted in the poem and how Propertius' amatory discourse produces an image of the elegiac mistress as the object of male fantasies of erotic domination — despite the apparent reversal of gender roles in the poem.

>   Qualis Thesea iacuit cedente carina
>   languida desertis Cnosia litoribus;
>   qualis et accubuit primo Cepheia somno
>   libera iam duris cotibus Andromede;
> 5   nec minus assiduis Edonis fessa choreis
>   qualis in herboso concidit Apidano:
>   talis visa mihi mollem spirare quietem
>   Cynthia non certis nixa caput manibus,
>   ebria cum multo traherem vestigia Baccho,
> 10   et quaterent sera nocte facem pueri.
>   hanc ego, nondum etiam sensus deperditus omnis
>   molliter impresso conor adire toro;
>   et quamvis duplici correptum ardore iuberent
>   hac Amor hac Liber, durus uterque deus,
> 15 subiecto leviter positam temptare lacerto
>   osculaque admota sumere et arma manu,
>   non tamen ausus eram dominae turbare quietem,
>   expertae metuens iurgia saevitiae;
>   sed sic intentis haerebam fixus ocellis,
> 20   Argus ut ignotis cornibus Inachidos.
>   et modo solvebam nostra de fronte corallas
>   ponebamque tuis, Cynthia, temporibus;
>   et modo gaudebam lapsos formare capillos;
>   nunc furtiva cavis poma dabam manibus;
> 25 omniaque ingrato largibar munera somno,
>   munera de prono saepe voluta sinu;
>   et quotiens raro duxti suspiria motu,
>   obstupui vano credulus auspicio,
>   ne qua tibi insolitos portarent visa timores,
> 30   neve quis invitam cogeret esse suam:
>   donec diversas praecurrens luna fenestras,

```
           luna moraturis sedula luminibus,
        compositos levibus radiis patefecit ocellos.
           sic ait in molli fixa toro cubitum:
35      'tandem te nostro referens iniuria lecto
           alterius clausis expulit e foribus?
        namque ubi longa meae consumpsti tempora noctis,
           languidus exactis, ei mihi, sideribus?
        o utinam talis perducas, improbe, noctes,
40         me miseram qualis semper habere iubes!
        nam modo purpureo fallebam stamine somnum,
           rursus et Orpheae carmine, fessa, lyrae;
        interdum leviter mecum deserta querebar
           externo longas saepe in amore moras:
45      dum me iucundis lapsam sopor impulit alis.
           illa fuit lacrimis ultima cura meis.'
```

[As on the lonely beach Ariadne lay, fainting while Theseus' keel receded; or like Andromeda free at last from her rocky prison, her limbs relaxed in the first flush of sleep. She looked like a girl from Thrace exhausted from her Bacchic dancing, sunk to rest by the grassy banks of the river. There she lay, breathing gently, all at peace, with her head lying on unresisting hands. Then I staggered in, dragging my footsteps, drunk as a lord, in the wee hours, when the torch was burning low. And I had an urge—I still had some of my faculties left—to tiptoe quietly up to the bed where she lay. I was growing hot, set on fire by a double flame, drink and desire, an insistent pair of masters. Have a go, they said,—put your arms around her softly—come closer—now then—kiss her—take her by storm. But I didn't dare disturb her when she looked so quiet and peaceful; she's a devil when she's roused, as I know too well. So I just stood there watching, all eyes—like Argus gazing with some surprise at Io's horns. And then I took off the garland I still had on from the party, and put it gently on your sleeping brows. If your hair was out of place, I lovingly rearranged it, and smuggled you apples in my cupped hands. But you were far away—these gifts meant nothing to you, and they rolled from your lap time and again to the floor. And when you stirred at times and heaved a sigh, I stood transfixed with empty apprehension. I thought you sighed at a nightmare, full of strange horrors, or a man who tried to take you against your will. And then at last the passing moon shone full in your window, the busybody moon, outstaying its welcome. The pale light of its beams unshuttered your sleeping eyes. . . . And off she started, propped up in bed on her elbow: "So you've come at last, and only because that other woman has thrown you out and closed the doors against you."]

As Leo Curran observes, 1.3 does not establish any narrative context for the poem but instead launches immediately into the world of myth and legend.[26] From the outset, Propertius introduces us to Cynthia by comparing her with famed mythological heroines and thereby implicitly compares the speaker with the corresponding male heroes. Although scholars have been in accord about the elevation of tone and language in the opening lines and about how Propertius transports the elegiac lovers to the exotic and idealized world of myth, there has been a good deal of disagreement about the extent of the erotic implications in the language of the first three couplets. Lyne and Allen view Cynthia in these couplets as an entirely idealized image of mythic beauty who "remains in a world beyond time."[27] Although both Curran and Harmon mention some of the sexual connotations in the vision of the sleeping Cynthia, R. J. Baker, in his article "Beauty and the Beast in Propertius 1.3," maintains that the first six lines of the poem contain "an undercurrent of sexual reference in these mythological *exempla* which Propertius fully intended readers of this poem to recognize."[28] In particular, Baker points out the sexual connotations of such words as *iacuit* (line 1), *languida* (line 2), and *accubuit* (line 3).

Although Baker does not romanticize the vision of Cynthia in the beginning couplets as much as other commentators on the poem, he too fails to provide any gender analysis of the ways desire is expressed in the poem. Indeed, all of the approaches to the poem seem to be limited by an identification with the perspective and values of the male narrator.[29] Criticism on the poem has not even attempted to link the so-called "idealization" of Cynthia to a particularly masculine point of view. I want to explore how the "woman in a text" is a projection of male fantasy and desire and moreover reflects male stereotypes about women which deny them agency and autonomy.

We may begin by analyzing the specific comparisons of the sleeping Cynthia with mythical heroines and how they express aspects of peculiarly masculine views of "ideal" amatory relations. Daniel Harmon points out that images of rest (*languida*) link the three *exempla* to one another and that "it is not merely sleep, but varying degrees or attitudes of sleep which invite comparison with Cynthia."[30] Harmon, however, does not consider the implications of the speaker clearly relishing the opportunity Cynthia's sleeping state offers him to create his version of idealized fantasies of his mistress. In the first *exemplum*, the speaker compares his sleeping mistress with Ariadne as she sleeps on the shore — unaware that she has been abandoned by Theseus: *Qualis Thesea iacuit cedente carina / languida desertis Cnosia litoribus* [As on the lonely beach Ariadne lay, fainting while Theseus' keel receded] (lines 1 and 2). Here the speaker imagines his mistress in a state of helplessness which allows him to play the role of rescuer. Indeed, in the myth Bacchus comes and rescues Ariadne from the deserted shore. As the drunken lover, the speaker's connection with Bacchus is clear. Curran observes that "like Bacchus, Propertius is on fire with love . . . the mention of Bacchus himself in 9 and 14 is, of course, not inconsistent with the identification of Propertius with the god; indeed the explicit reference confirms the identification."[31] The implication is that the image of the stranded and helpless woman evokes desire in the male lover. Moreover, the speaker's arousal seems to depend on turning his "real" mistress into a static, pictorial object he can watch without any resistance or interference from "reality." The object of desire he imagines, both in the myth and in the narrative context of the poem, lacks agency of her own.

The second *exemplum* of Andromeda's release by her lover Perseus continues the theme of the male lover delivering a defenseless mistress from danger and abandonment: *qualis et accubuit primo Cepheia somno / libera iam duris cotibus Andromede* [And as Andromeda freed at last from her rocky prison, her limbs relaxed in the first flush of sleep] (lines 3 and 4). As both Curran and Harmon point out, Propertius' use of *accubuit* in line 3 has the usual sexual connotation. Thus, the linkage of the release of Andromeda with the sexual consummation of her marriage to Perseus again connects female helplessness and captivity to male fantasies of erotic fulfillment. This association of the sleeping heroine with erotic fantasy culminates in the image in the third *exemplum* of the frenzied Maenad who collapses in exhaustion onto the grass after incessant dances: *nec minus assiduis Edonis fessa choreis / qualis in herboso concidit Apidano* [no less she looked like a girl from Thrace exhausted by her Bacchic dancing, sunk to rest by the grassy banks of the river] (lines 5 and 6). This last *exemplum* deviates from the pattern of the two previous ones in that there is no allusion to a male figure corresponding to Theseus or Perseus; the Maenad is "self-sufficient in her ecstasy."[32] Despite the implication of the Bacchante's active expression of desire and her autonomy, the speaker's vision of the Maenad seems to resemble the speaker's own drunken state more than Cynthia's sleeping condition. The three *exempla* become progressively more overt in their sexual connotations and thus suggest a heightening of the speaker's arousal as he constructs fantasies of his mistress held captive by his imagination. Cynthia seems most desirable to the speaker as long as she remains a *fantasy*—a static projection of his own desires. As Curran comments,

"There is a certain static quality about the world of the heroines, which is only in part owing to the fact that they are all recumbent. They have the stability, permanence, and immutability of works of art, whether or not Propertius had particular paintings or statues in mind."[33] Curran's suggestion that the images of mythical heroines are statuelike and that later on in the poem the speaker's offer of gifts to the sleeping Cynthia "might as well be . . . offerings before the statue of a woman or a goddess" is entirely apt. Curran, however, does not question the assumptions implicit in the male lover's "drawn-out gaze." Although both Curran and Harmon acknowledge the "unreciprocal confrontation of watcher and watched . . . gazing and being gazed at,"[34] they privilege this process of specularization and do not explore the implications *for the woman* of being subjected to the gaze of the male.

In the second section of the poem (lines 11–20), where the speaker attempts to approach the "real" Cynthia as she sleeps, he nonetheless continues to treat her as an object of erotic fantasy. The prospect of encounter only evokes another mythic comparison, one that heightens the expression of the speaker's fantasies of domination and control over a helpless, captive mistress. The speaker describes himself staring at Cynthia as Argus gazed on Io. Curran sees the process of gazing in the relationship of Argus and Io as an expression of intimacy.[35] This view suggests that intimacy is primarily a matter of male protectiveness toward a vulnerable and defenseless female. Neither Curran nor Harmon considers the implications of control and captivity in the picture of Io being watched *and* guarded by Argus. Later in the poem, the speaker expresses his fears about Cynthia being "taken" by another man as he imagines what Cynthia might be dreaming: *et quotiens raro duxti suspiria motu, / obstupui vano credulus auspicio, / ne qua tibi insolitos portarent visa timores, / neve quis invitam cogeret esse suam* [And when you stirred at times and heaved a sigh, I stood transfixed with empty apprehension; I thought you sighed at a nightmare, full of strange horrors, or a man who tried to take you against your will] (lines 27–30). In view of the speaker's earlier attempts to approach his sleeping mistress in a way that suggests an "aroused physical state," it is quite possible to read the speaker's concern about Cynthia's dream as a projection of his own sexual desires and intentions.

Scholars tend to emphasize how charming it is that the speaker approaches his mistress so timidly, but they fail to explore how his mythical, that is to say, *idealized* depiction of himself as rescuer, protector, and ultimately captor of his mistress devalues the woman and denies her subjectivity and autonomy. Moreover, the speaker's gestures of arranging garlands on Cynthia's head, rearranging her hair, and trying to place apples into her hands do not, I believe, "increase the feeling of intimacy and tenderness" as Curran thinks. These gestures, rather, reinforce a portrayal of Cynthia as a mannequinlike figure; the speaker arranges her as an artist might arrange a still life. In addition, the eroticism suggested by the images of apples[36] furthers the idea that turning Cynthia into a pictorial object is linked to the sexual arousal of the male lover.

Indeed, the speaker's imagination comes alive when his mistress is asleep, when she exists as a *tabula rasa* upon which he can inscribe his desires. Ironically, in 1.3 Propertius gives Cynthia a voice of her own; in fact, she has the "last word" in the poem. But when she awakens and is presented as a flesh and blood woman with desires and prerogatives of her own, her voice becomes an abrupt, unpleasant intrusion into the rich inner life of the narrator. She is a shrew who was most desirable when she was completely subjected to the gaze of the male narrator—with no voice or agency of her own.

By giving us Cynthia's own words rather than letting the speaker narrate them, Propertius is able to dramatize the narrator's experience of reality clashing with myth. The transformation of Cynthia from an idealized object of beauty to a hysterical female is shocking; Cynthia's diatribe against her drunken lover seems not so much an indictment of his irresponsible behavior but shows, dramatically, how Cynthia's particular form of discourse confines her within the banalities of circumstance and everyday existence and sets her apart from the speaker's own highly imaginative poetic practice. Curran's view of Cynthia's "outburst on awakening" reflects the unquestioning attitude toward the perspective of the male speaker which has dominated criticism on the poem: "Propertius had fancied himself a Bacchus or a Perseus, but in Cynthia's eyes he is only a disappointed Lothario, seeking solace with his second choice for the evening. Cynthia is, of course, only drawing her own inferences about how Propertius has spent his evening, but [he] is given no chance to deny his charges and has already admitted that he has arrived very late at night from an elaborate and bibulous party. The initial vision, with its romantic dignity and its augury of success, has been almost completely destroyed."[37]

Such a view seems to privilege inevitably the way desire is constituted and expressed by the male lover and is thus unable to question the stereotypical portrayals of the woman put forth by the speaker. Curran, like Propertius, has entrapped Cynthia within the unfortunate roles of being *either* a woman who evokes desire through her helplessness and passivity *or* a shrewish nag who destroys the lover's lofty visions of beauty and tenderness. By ending the poem with Cynthia's complaints, Propertius leaves us with the disappointing realities of amatory relations—realities that are vocalized by a woman who seems to fulfill the stereotype of the rancorous wife scolding her man for his unruly, irresponsible ways while she reminds him, in her mock-tragic tone, what a victim she has become. Cynthia's "absence" (her sleep) provides the speaker with the opportunity to create images of her projected from fantasies of domination which are linked to his sexual arousal. In like manner, Cynthia's "actual" absence in *Elegy* 1.11 gives rise to the narrator's fantasies about her—fantasies that reveal a more overt attempt to objectify her and control her sexuality.

In my discussion of the poem, I shall argue that by identifying Cynthia with nature, with "uncivilized" urges and passions, Propertius relegates her to a sphere that is traditionally regarded as inferior.[38] Indeed, one of the chief *topoi* in the poems of both Catullus and Propertius is the complaint about the tendency of their mistresses to lack control over their seemingly insatiable sexual desires—desires that, of course, require their men to keep them in line. As Maria Wyke has pointed out, the sexual promiscuity of women is a conventional *topos* in the invective tradition against women.[39] Moreover, from the period after the rise of Rome to imperial status, a burgeoning of moral discourses associated female sexual impropriety with social and political disorder.[40] I will show that in *Elegy* 1.11, Propertius identifies Cynthia with the disruptive and dangerous sensuality that was considered a threat to the perpetuation of Roman cultural values.

Elegy 1.11

Ecquid te mediis cessantem, Cynthia, Bais,
    qua iacet Herculeis semita litoribus,
et modo Thesproti mirantem subdita regno
    proxima Misenis aequora nobilibus,
5   nostri cura subit memores, a, ducere noctes?
    ecquis in extremo restat amore locus?
an te nescio quis simulatis ignibus hostis
    sustulit e nostris, Cynthia, carminibus?
atque utinam mage te remis confisa minutis
10 parvula Lucrina cumba moretur aqua,
aut teneat clausam tenui Teuthrantis in unda
    alternae facilis cedere lympha manu,
quam vacet alterius blandos audire susurros
    molliter in tacito litore compositam!
15 ut solet amoto labi custode puella,
    perfida communis nec meminisse deos:

> non quia perspecta non es mihi cognita fama,
>   sed quod in hac omnis parte timetur amor.
> ignosces igitur, si quid tibi triste libelli
> 20   attulerint nostri: culpa timoris erit.
> an mihi nunc maior carae custodia matris?
>   aut sine te vitae cura sit ulla meae?
> tu mihi sola domus, tu, Cynthia, sola parentes,
>   omnia tu nostrae tempora laetitiae.
> 25 seu tristis veniam seu contra laetus amicis,
>   quicquid ero, dicam 'Cynthia causa fuit.'
> tu modo quam primum corruptas desere Baias:
>   multis ista dabunt litora discidium,
> litora quae fuerunt castis inimica puellis:
>   a pereant Baiae, crimen amoris, aquae!

[While you, Cynthia, are relaxing in the midst of Baiae, where Hercules' causeway stretches along the shore, even now admiring the waters that are subjected to Thesprotus' realm, bordering on noble Misenum. Does concern come over you, to spend nights mindful of me? Is there room left for me at the edge of your love? Or has some unknown enemy, with simulated ardor, carried you away, Cynthia, from my poems? I would much prefer that some small boat, trusting to its tiny oars, detained you on the Lucrine lake, or that the water were holding you enclosed in Teuthras' thin wave, the water, willing to give way to your alternating arms, than you, softly stretched on the silent beach, have leisure for the flattering whispers of another man. As is the rule: Once the guardian is removed, the girl lapses, and faithlessly, no longer remembers mutual gods. Not that I do not know your proven honor, but in this place all love is feared. Thus forgive me, if my letters bring you sadness; my anxious fear shall be at fault. Could I be a better guard of my own dear mother? Or would I, without you, have any concern for my own life? You are my only parents, my only home, Cynthia, you are every moment of my joy! Whether I appear sad to my friends or joyful, whatever I am, I will say, "Cynthia has been the cause." As soon as possible, leave corrupted Baiae: to many lovers these shores mean separation, shores so hostile to chaste girls: Oh, may the waters of Baiae perish, love's corruption!]

In this poem, the narrator expresses his anxious fears about his mistress' trip to the fashionable Roman resort of Baiae—a place with a reputation for encouraging indulgence in sensual and erotic pleasure. The speaker fantasizes about Cynthia in Baiae and imagines her not only as part of the lush, sensual landscape itself but also as unable to withstand erotic temptation and uphold the *sancta fides* of their romantic union. As John Warden points out, addresses in Propertius create the illusion of listening in on private speech.[41] The speaker's abrupt, urgent opening address to Cynthia, which throws us into the middle of an ongoing argument, creates from the beginning an impression of dramatic vitality and immediacy. This sense of ongoing drama is heightened by the image of Cynthia already "in the midst of the pleasures of Baiae" (*mediis Bais*). But despite the illusion of intimate dialogue and of a dramatic situation here, in the second line of the poem we are plunged into highly embellished poetic language and a complicated syntax that suggest we are in a poetic rather than a geographical landscape.

Indeed, from the speaker's dramatic opening and his reference to a real place, we may expect a detailed description of the pleasures that Baiae offers. Instead, he introduces Baiae to us in language that draws our attention away from narrative to the realm of imagination and myth. The mention of Hercules at line 2 as the builder of the causeway at Baiae and the allusion to the "realm of Thesprotus" (a mythical king whose country is associated with an entrance to the underworld) to describe Baiae's waters show that the speaker is, from the outset, more interested in his imagination of Baiae than he is in presenting a realistic picture of it.

In light of Baiae's reputation as a corrupter of *puellae*, it is curious that the speaker emphasizes the sensually appealing aspects of the place and lingers on the images that produce wonder rather than revulsion. Despite the speaker's fears about what Cynthia may be doing at Baiae, he clearly derives pleasure from her absence, in the opportunity it gives him to fantasize about her in a new place. Separation and the possibility of loss give the speaker the opportunity to re-create Cynthia imaginatively and to elevate and embellish her by linking her to a mythological realm.

At line 5, the speaker shifts abruptly from Thesprotus' mythical realm to a passionate query of Cynthia to remember him and to hold a place in the corner of her heart for him. The speaker presents himself as the unhappy lover asking his mistress for even the smallest tokens of love. His devaluation of his imagined rival according to the only criterion that really matters for lovers — depth of passion — contradicts his presentation of himself as helpless and vulnerable. The speaker clearly has weapons his rival lacks, and he is clever in suggesting that Cynthia's fame depends on his willingness to immortalize her. The way the words *nostris carminibus* enclose Cynthia's name in line 8 shows the fusion of the speaker's poems and Cynthia's name and also implies that the figure of the *puella* to whom he speaks is less a woman he is wooing than a *subject* for his writing.

The mention of *nostris carminibus* leads directly to the speaker's evocation of Cynthia on the Lucrine lake. The speaker fantasizes Cynthia as he would like her to be, away from the realities of potential corruption and temptation, held (*teneat*) and enclosed (*clausam*) in his imagination. These verbs of holding and enclosing recall the speaker's fantasies in 1.3 of his mistress in a state of idealized captivity. But in 1.11, Cynthia's absence permits the speaker's imagination free rein. He envisions what he would like Cynthia to be doing at Baiae and yet fears these same visons. In the first case, the speaker pictures Cynthia alone in a small boat, enclosed by water that yields to her arms as they move in alternating motions. Although the speaker sees Cynthia isolated and protected—her sexuality in bounds—he nonetheless describes her sensuality and seductiveness. A pattern similar to the one in 1.3 emerges here: the image of the mistress detained, confined, and protected leads to a heightening of the speaker's sexual arousal. Indeed, in lines 13–16 the speaker's fantasy of Cynthia in the middle of an attempted seduction suggests this intensification of the speaker's excitement. The sensual immediacy with which the speaker describes Cynthia stretched out on the beach, listening leisurely to the whispers of another man, has an air of voyeuristic titillation. It seems that Cynthia's erotic charms overshadow the moral implications of her imagined infidelities. In fact, the speaker's rapt absorption in the sensually appealing fantasies of his beloved with another man points to an autoeroticism that fuels both his literary and sexual imaginations.

But as in 1.3, here the speaker casts Cynthia in the stereotypical role of the faithless, sexually unrestrained female who needs to be monitored and controlled. Immediately after becoming carried away with his fantasies of a potentially promiscuous Cynthia, the speaker vilifies women in general for their tendencies to transgress the norms of female behavior: "As is the rule: once the guardian is removed, the girl lapses, and faithlessly, no longer remembers mutual gods" (lines 15 and 16). By invoking *communis deos* in the context of female sexual transgression, the speaker implies that female sexuality poses potential dangers to commonly accepted views of social and political order. As Maria Wyke argues, the elegiac lover's avowed position of servitude toward his mistress must not be taken to imply female empowerment. But Wyke does put forth the view that elegists "explore . . . the concept of male dependency."[42] I think such a view does not take into account the degree of manipulation and posturing in the elegiac stance of servitude toward the mistress.

As we saw in 1.3, the speaker appears to be titillated by imagining his mistress in a state of helpless captivity, and in 1.11 he is aroused by fantasizing about her possible transgressions. These two poems dramatize a polarization of women—"into the chaste and the depraved,"[43] a polarization that makes the representation of female sexuality a projection of male desire. In 1.3, the posturing in the speaker's stance of servitude toward Cynthia is suggested through mythical *exempla* that emphasize female helplessness and dependence on men. And in 1.11, the speaker presents a rather stereotypical picture of female sexual misconduct. In both poems, the elegiac mistress is an object of erotic fantasy and fertile material for poetic production. Thus, the speaker's apparently servile position can be read, at least in part, as a strategy of manipulation to promote his own artistic fame.

Indeed, at line 17 the speaker shifts abruptly from his moralistic tone about how women need guardians to keep their sexuality in bounds to a mood of supplication, as he asks Cynthia to forgive him. The speaker's convoluted double negatives at line 17 suggest a confusion in his attitudes toward Cynthia. On the one hand, he flatters Cynthia by telling her that her *fama* is unquestionable; on the other hand, the use of *fama*, especially in light of Cynthia's imagined infidelities, can also imply a bad reputation. Thus, declaring that Cynthia's *fama* is well known to the speaker may also cast doubt on her honor, by questioning her transgressions at Baiae. The ambiguity in the meaning of *fama* (good or bad reputation) suggests the speaker's binary images of his mistress. Moreover, *perspecta* at line 17 conveys a sense of active scrutiny rather than passive knowledge, which reflects how the speaker's imagination has been scrutinizing Cynthia's reputation.

The fear the speaker expresses at line 18 that "all love is feared in Baiae" recalls his earlier fear that some "unknown enemy" has already snatched Cynthia from his poems. The speaker's manipulative strategies toward his mistress are all but transparent; he implies that her *fama* (good or bad) depends on the continuation of her position as his mistress. The speaker's offer (or threat) to confer *fama* functions as a very persuasive argument for Cynthia's continued faithfulness, but it also suggests a reversal of the elegiac balance of power in which the male lover is subservient to his mistress. The speaker, essentially, suggests that Cynthia offer herself to him as *materia* for the continuation of his poetic practice. His fear of losing her to other suitors at Baiae seems to be as much a fear about Cynthia's *name* being snatched from his literary productions as it is a fear of her being snatched from his life.

We can see the speaker's manipulations and convoluted logic in his claim that the *culpa* is solely his—his ability to imagine vividly the moral transgressions Cynthia commits. Cynthia's absence, like her sleep in 1.3, provides the *tabula rasa* on which the speaker can project his fantasies and desires. Taking all the moral blame on himself—in light of his earlier allusion to the moral laxity of *puellae*—can be understood as part of his strategy of self-effacement toward his mistress. The speaker's desire to renew a poetic practice in which Cynthia will not only have a crucial role but from which she will gain praise *or* condemnation is the most persuasive argument the speaker can use to get his mistress back and thus increase the likelihood of his own *fama* as well.

The speaker's strategy of manipulation continues through his comparison of Cynthia with his own mother (lines 21–24). In this passage, the roles the speaker assigns to himself and his mistress reflect a profound confusion in the way gender relations are constructed in this poem. The image of the speaker as the *custodia* of his mother recalls the earlier implications of male protectiveness expressed in the images of containment associated with Cynthia. But more important is the way the speaker turns his mistress into his mother. Before this, Cynthia was associated with an indulgence in sensual pleasure which seemed to transgress appropriate social conduct for women. Now, Cynthia is the desexualized, infinitely nurturing mother who, of course, could not possibly abandon her dependent, desolate son. This shift from the woman as dangerously unrestrained to woman as chaste, fertile, and selfless again points up the polarization of women into good and bad, virtuous and depraved.

The speaker, however, transforms Cynthia not only into his mother but into his father as well, and as both, she is stripped of her gender altogether and of any trace of sexuality. Moreover, it is interesting that this passage recalls Catullus' Poem 72 in which the speaker declares that he loves Lesbia *as* a father loves a son: *dilexi tum te non tantum ut vulgus amicam, / sed pater ut gnatos diligit et generos* [I loved you then not only as the common sort love a mistress, but as a father loves his sons and sons-in-law] (lines 3 and 4). Propertius reverses Catullus by comparing the lover not with the parent but with the child. Furthermore, Propertius' speaker does not merely compare his relationship to Cynthia with the filial love between parents and children. He says that Cynthia *is* his parents; it would be difficult not to see the hyperbole in such a statement. What could be more guilt inducing than telling Cynthia that she is as responsible for the speaker's life as parents are for those of their children? The implications of nurturance in equating Cynthia with his parents and making his survival depend on that nurturance reinforce the importance of Cynthia's role in the continuation of the speaker's poetic practice.

The sense in which the speaker considers Cynthia crucial to both the private and public aspects of his life is evident in his declaration that Cynthia is the cause of both what he is and how he appears to others (lines 25 and 26). The speaker's overriding concern seems to be for *Cynthia* as a *name in a text*. It is the speaker's own text—his speaking—that *makes* Cynthia the reason for his existence and the basis of how others see him. The speaker's language—his text—causes him to be what he is and controls the image he puts forth to the world. The speaker does not merely report that he informs his friends about Cynthia's crucial role in his life. He emphasizes the role of language in conveying that information and thus reveals his self-conscious awareness of his own active role in creating images of himself and his mistress.

Moreover, Cynthia's existence—real or imagined—is defined exclusively in relation to the speaker. She is a projection of the male lover's moods and thoughts—indeed, of his very identity. One of the most important aspects of feminist theory has been a critique of the assumption underlying Western philosophical discourse [44] that the woman is merely man's *other*, a mirror of his masculinity, and that she can never achieve the status of subject, at least for or by herself. Applied to Cynthia's position in 1.3, this point of view reduces her to a foil for the male speaker.[45]

In addition, Jessica Benjamin's study of the oedipal model in her analysis of gender and erotic domination [46] is useful for understanding the polarized images of the mistress in 1.11, where, for the speaker, the mistress is both seductress and nurturing mother. Benjamin argues that "on the psychic level, the oedipal repudiation of the mother splits her into the debased and the idealized objects."[47] Furthermore, Benjamin observes that this split denies to the woman recognition of her own subjectivity. Her comments on this point, I believe, help to illuminate how male desire is constructed in 1.11. "The problem is that using the wife-mother as a prop for autonomy threatens to reduce her to a mere extension of the self. . . . This is a version of the contradiction we saw in erotic domination, the fear that we have destroyed or wholly objectified the other whom we need. It is also another version of the oedipal model: wanting to devalue and control the other while still drawing sustenance from her, *wanting to keep mother in captivity* and yet alive and strong [my emphasis]."[48] The image of the captive woman whose separate identity is never recognized, who is devalued and objectified *as a woman* yet needed for emotional and creative nurturance, seems to be a crucial element in the way the mistress is depicted in both 1.3 and 1.11.

In the last four lines of 1.11, the speaker returns to the moralistic, paternalistic tone he adopted earlier (lines 27–30). The speaker's abrupt shift from imagining Cynthia as the chaste, nurturing woman to evoking the moral laxity of *puellae* in general suggests the polarized view of the good and the bad woman. The speaker blames Baiae for corrupting the chastity of young women, but the angry tone of his moralistic railings recalls his earlier allusion to the tendency women have to stray once their guardians are removed. The speaker cannot expect us to believe, literally, that the shores of Baiae are the source of corruption. They merely provide the opportunity for women to do what is customary (*ut solet*) for them: lapsing into depravity if they are not under the control and watchful eye of a man.

Moreover, there is irony in the speaker's use of the word *crimen* in the last line of the poem. *Crimen* is in apposition to *aquae Baiae;* but earlier, the speaker admitted his own anxious imaginings to be at fault. It is the speaker who evoked the seductiveness of the waters of Baiae and vividly conjured up fantasies of a *crimen* at Baiae. In fact, the speaker's *crimen* produced the captivating images of his beloved through which the speaker and his mistress will both be remembered. The only *crimen* is that projected from the speaker's imagination and which, ironically, makes him desire Cynthia more. The titillation in fantasizing about the potential seduction of his mistress at Baiae leads the speaker to vilify women in general but, at the same time, to express his urgent desire for Cynthia to return to him. The speaker's depiction of his mistress according to binary views of women as *either* virtuous *or* corrupt offers little possibility for women to be considered as subjects in their own right.

Indeed, the male lover's position of servitude helps to facilitate the gender polarities that inform the way amatory relations are portrayed in Propertius' elegiac texts. The dependent, servile stance of the lover which gives rise to the image of the *domina* creates a hierarchical configuration of lover and beloved which is based on relations of power. I have tried to show that despite the alienation of the male narrator from customary masculine pursuits and from positions of power, Propertius nonetheless transfers many conventional attitudes and assumptions about women to the expression of male desire. *Elegies* 1.3 and 1.11 in particular, through their polarized representations of the elegiac mistress, suggest the entrapment of the woman within a discursive practice that preserves her object status and places her in a symbolic order structured around male fantasies of control over women's autonomy and sexuality. Much of the criticism on Propertian elegy has, unfortunately, tended to accept the male lover's "idealized" images of his mistress as simply a part of the genre and has failed to question the implications of the lover's mythologizing for the way women are both read and represented.

CHAPTER FOUR

Ovid's *Amores*

Women, Violence, and Voyeurism

We must not think that by
saying yes to sex,
one says no to power.
—Michel Foucault

IN THE PREVIOUS CHAPTER, I discussed how Propertius inscribes his mistress as a "woman in a text" and subordinates her role as beloved to her role as narrative *materia* for the poet's writing. Unlike Ovid's *amator*, however, Propertius' narrator never removes the mask of elegiac lover, never abandons the elegiac fiction of sexual role inversion, in which women are portrayed as dominant and men as subservient. Moreover, the *amator* in Propertian elegy maintains the fiction of the devoted, dependent, passive lover and the ideal of *fides* upon which that fiction depends. Ovid, on the other hand, while exploiting the elegiac convention of the image of the *amator* as *servus amoris*, reveals, even in the opening poem in his collection of elegies, that this image is merely a rhetorical posture, a ruse for seduction and manipulation. Thus, by implicating his *amator* in a multitude of contradictions and letting us "see through" his manipulations and exploitations of women, Ovid shatters the fiction of the male narrator as enslaved and the female narrative subject as his enslaver.

Ovid's attitudes toward women and his narrator's program of erotic deception and conquest in the *Amores* have prompted a good deal of attention in recent Ovidian criticism.[1] The tradition of scholarship in Ovid's amatory works,[2] however, has tended to dismiss the *amator*'s attitudes and practices as merely a part of Ovid's strategy to entertain his audiences with his ingenious wit.³ Ovidian scholars have, traditionally, been charmed and amused by the *amator*'s clever manipulations and deceptive amatory strategies but have not, for the most part, considered to what degree Ovid's *Amores* is, as Mary-Kay Gamel asserts, a "gendered text" requiring a "female reading."⁴

Indeed, recent feminist critics have contended that Ovid's poetry ought to be read as a critique of the competitive and exploitative nature of *amor*. Among feminist interpretations of Ovid there is, of course, disagreement about how to read his apparent valorization of traditional male domination over women. Both Leslie Cahoon and Amy Richlin have expressed horror at "all the black Ovidian travesties of love" which appear in his amatory texts.⁵ In her essay "Reading Ovid's Rapes," Richlin argues that Ovid is a pornographer who encourages the reader to enjoy violence inflicted on women. She points up the horror in the intersection of pleasure and violence in Ovid's texts and in his representation of the "female as the site of violence." ⁶ In her view, Ovid's pornographic model "offers no exit from gender hierarchy."

Leo Curran, on the other hand, argues that Ovid's insight into the suffering of women victimized by male domination reflects a sympathy for the plight of women.⁷ In a similar vein, Leslie Cahoon, Mary-Kay Gamel, and Julie Hemker argue that Ovid's presentation of sexual violence and the exploitation of women is a complex literary strategy that serves to unmask and critique the brutality inherent in amatory relations. In this chapter, I shall argue that by provoking us into a gradual uneasiness at the consequences of domination, Ovid's poems invite us to question the perspectives of a lover who espouses and practices conquest and deception as a way of life. To explore how Ovid's poems not only expose the destructive aspects of *amor* but also reveal the mechanics of male discourses of power and domination over women, I shall examine *Amores* 1.1, 1.3, 1.5, and 1.7. My analysis will also focus on the inscription of gender in the visual figuration of masculine and feminine positions in *Amores* 1.3, 1.5, and 1.7. I will argue that the elegiac mistress is turned into the *object* of the narrator's voyeuristic gaze and that the configuration of seer and seen revolves on a pattern of male dominance and female abasement, despite the apparent reversal of traditional gender roles in elegiac poetry.

Amores 1.1

We see from the programmatic first poem that Ovid moves from the Propertian fiction of the mistress as *domina* to a blatant portrayal of her as *materia*, as a signifier of the male lover's aesthetic choices and poetic practices. Ovid's collection of elegies opens with the narrator announcing his change in status from epic poet to a writer of elegies.

> Arma gravi numero violentaque bella parabam
>   edere, materia conveniente modis.
> par erat inferior versus; risisse Cupido
>   dicitur atque unum surripuisse pedem.
> 5 'quis tibi, saeve puer, dedit hoc in carmina iuris?
>   Pieridum vates, non tua, turba sumus.
> quid, si praeripiat flavae Venus arma Minervae,
>   ventilet accensas flava Minerva faces?
> quis probet in silvis Cererem regnare iugosis,
> 10   ege pharetratae virginis arva coli?
> crinibus insignem quis acuta cuspide Phoebum
>   instruat, Aoniam Marte movente lyram?
> sunt tibi magna, puer, nimiumque potentia regna:
>   cur opus adfectas ambitiose novum?
> 15 an, quod ubique, tuum est? tua sunt Heliconia tempe?
>   vix etiam Phoebo iam lyra tuta sua est?
> cum bene surrexit versu nova pagina primo,
>   attenuat nervos proximus ille meos.
> nec mihi materia est numeris levioribus apta,
> 20   aut puer aut longas compta puella comas.'
> questus eram, pharetra cum protinus ille soluta
>   legit in exitium spicula facta meum
> lunavitque genu sinuosum fortiter arcum
>   'quod'que 'canas, vates, accipe' dixit 'opus.'
> 25 me miserum! certas habuit puer ille sagittas:
>   uror, et in vacuo pectore regnat Amor.
> sex mihi surgat opus numeris, in quinque residat;
>   ferrea cum vestris bella valeta modis.
> cingere litorea flaventia tempora myrto,
> 30   Musa per undenos emodulanda pedes.

[Arms, warfare, violence—I was about to produce a regular epic, with verse-form to match—hexameters, of course. But Cupid (they say) with a snicker snatched one foot from each alternate line. "Nasty boy, I said, who gave you jurisdiction over meters? We poets come under the Muses, we're not in your crowd. What if Venus took over the weapons of blond Minerva, while blond Minerva fanned the flames of passion? Who'd approve of Ceres ruling over hilly forests, or the quiver-wearing Virgin safeguarding crops? Who'd approve of Apollo arrayed for battle with a sharp spear, while Mars played Apollo's lyre? You've got your own dominion, boy, and, in fact, you've got too much power; why do you go after a new task even more ambitious? Or is your power everywhere, is Helicon yours, is Apollo's lyre scarcely safe anymore? When a new page has sprung up, with a good opening line, then the next line takes away my power. I don't have a suitable theme for your frivolous meter, neither a boy, nor a girl with coiffured hair." Immediately after I complained, he opened his quiver, chose arrows designed for my destruction, bent the winding bow firmly against his knee, and said "Poet, you want something to sing, take that." Wretched me! That boy had unerring arrows: I'm on fire now, and Love rules over an empty heart. So let my verse rise with six measures, and drop down to five. Farewell to cruel wars, and to the meters that go along with them. Come, Muse, wreathe your blond hair with myrtle, singing in meters of eleven.]

At first glance the poem appears to be part of a traditional Callimachean polemic on the debate between the conflicting merits of literary styles and the values they embody. As his predecessors did, Ovid seems to be defending his position as a writer of elegy rather than epic. But the first line of the poem, as critics have pointed out, recalls the first line of the *Aeneid*. Alison Keith, for example, reads the allusion to Virgil's epic as implying that Ovid is asserting that his poetry "is of such a calibre as to challenge comparison even with Virgil's epic."[8] This interpretation, however, does not take into account the irony in the speaker's apparent disavowal of epic themes. The narrator appears to be telling his audience about what he is *not* going to do in this collection of elegies. He is *not* going to write about arms, warfare, and violence. But that is precisely what he does write about; the epic themes of war and conquest will be played out on the amatory battlefield.[9] Ovid does not enter the Callimachean literary debate merely to show concern for his own artistic production but to demonstrate the congruence rather than the dissimilarity between epic and elegiac literary themes.

In the first couplet the narrator describes the epic themes he is forced to reject as *materia*. Here, *materia* is associated with *bella*, but in later poems (beginning with 1.3) it is equated with the *puella*. This parallel between *bella* and *puella* as the poet's *materia* reinforces an abiding connection in the elegies between the violent conquest perpetrated in war and the male lover's violent domination and devaluation of his mistress. Although *edere* in line 2 is used by the narrator to describe his literary production, it also has associations with procreation. The speaker produces or publishes his *materia* and fashions or begets a *puella* who will be at the service of his artistic needs.

Cupid's appearance in the second couplet of the poem is a tenuous one. Ovid appears to reverse the literary convention of divine epiphany by having the poet rather than the deity speak. Keith sees the role of Cupid here as one that performs "the function of poetic inspiration."[10] But there is no evidence in the poem either that the speaker is at all inspired to write or that Cupid is responsible for that inspiration. First, the narrator describes the process of becoming an elegiac poet in a casual and flippant manner that militates against a view of him as "inspired." Cupid simply came along and for no apparent reason except "for fun" (*risisse*) took away one of his metrical feet. The narrator's change occurs because of a metrical technicality. Second, the speaker's statement that Cupid "is said" (*dicitur*) to have laughed and stolen one of his feet produces a qualification that undermines the credibility of Cupid's existence and, moreover, distances the whole event from the speaker. He reports the event either as if it did not happen to him directly or as if it did not really happen at all. Ovid seems to be mocking the literary conceit of presenting divine epiphany as the origin of poetic inspiration. This is reinforced by the speaker's direct address to Cupid. It is the speaker, not the deity, who assumes rhetorical control; the *amator* uses the speech to Cupid to display his own literary talents and inventiveness. Immediately after Ovid's *amator* berates Cupid for asserting his authority in an area where he has no business (lines 5 and 6), he shows himself to be fascinated with his own poetic virtuosity as he launches into a long list of hypothetical examples of gods who might venture into areas and activities inappropriate to them (lines 7–16). As the speaker shows off his inventiveness in picturing, for example, Minerva and Venus changing places, he also throws into confusion traditional ideas about cosmology, about how the universe is ordered, and how categories of experience are defined. These images of gods taking over functions that belong to other gods not only set a tone of irreverence for the elegies but also bring into focus the narrator's own virtuosic ability to reverse traditional conceptions and imagine a world where things are not as we expect them to be.

Although Horace, Tibullus, and Propertius also use the *recusatio* we see here, they provide substantial reasons for resisting epic poetry, reasons that have to do with the compulsions of their personal emotional lives and with their commitment to an erotic ideal. Ovid, on the other hand, gives no alternative to *arma violentaque bella*. But that is because, for Ovid's *amator*, the erotic life is not significantly different from the warfare and violence that are depicted in epic poetry. Ovid reveals from the very first elegy in the collection that his narrator will exploit the rhetoric and conventions of elegiac discourse for his own selfish ends. Ovid's *amator* finds a *puella* to suit the requirements of his new meter—*materia conveniente modis*. The narrator claims to lack the *materia* requisite for his new poetic practice. This assertion of ineptitude on the speaker's part calls attention to the emotional vacuousness of the male lover who does not care for any particular *puella* but only for the way in which she may be used as literary *materia*. The *amator*'s own reference to his empty heart (line 26) is a reminder not so much of how art precedes emotion but of how emotion is a matter of artifice for him. Indeed the *materia* he needs for his meter is a *puella* whose long hair is described as *compta*. *Compta*, in connection with the *puella*, suggests the close association of the Ovidian elegiac mistress with poetic composition, with a style of writing.[11] But the desired *compta puella* also calls forth the image of the obedient woman with well-ordered hair, an image that depicts the elegiac mistress more as art-object than love-object and also emphasizes men's control over women's sexuality.

The woman's lack of specificity and her association with artistic production are reinforced when Cupid's arrows remedy the *amator*'s complaints. As Leslie Cahoon has pointed out, although the *amator* announces that he is on fire with *amor*, no specific woman emerges here.[12] Not only does the *amator* lack passion for any individual beloved, but I would argue that he displays no real passion at all. His first words after being struck by Cupid's arrows, *me miserum*, appropriate the standard rhetoric of the elegiac lover. Indeed, Ovid's *me miserum* recalls Propertius' *miserum me* in his opening elegy (1.1.1).[13] But the contexts for these declarations of amatory anguish are quite different. Propertius' *miserum me* occurs in the middle of a line in which the Propertian lover declares his captivity to Cynthia. Cynthia, not *me*, is the rhetorical focus of Propertius' opening line and defines the way the speaker presents himself in terms of his relationship to a particular *puella*. Ovid's placement of *me* before *miserum*, on the other hand, suggests that Ovid's *amator* is focused primarily on himself and on the benefits he hopes to gain from his new status as love poet. He adopts the appropriately elegiac emotion only for effect. The passion occurs in a vacuum (despite the *amator*'s claim to the contrary) as a literary convenience. Further, the incredulity of the speaker's wretched condition is sustained by his immediate concern in line 27 for the precise requirements of his meter. Unlike Propertius' *amator*, the Ovidian lover quickly abandons his outpouring of emotion and blatantly turns his attention to his literary concerns (*sex mihi surgat opus numeris, in quinque residat*). The use of the third-person subjunctive here, moreover, effects an authoritative tone that belies the speaker's self-proclaimed powerlessness.

Despite his claim that *Amor* has vanquished him (*et in vacuo pectore regnat Amor*), the poem concludes with the *amator*'s clearly exuberant acceptance of his *servitium*. That he invents the verb *emodulor* to describe the rise and fall of the elegiac meter reflects the extent to which the *amator* is fully in control of his poetic medium.[14] He bids farewell to *ferrea bella*, but his linkage of *Amor* with *regnat* suggests that the warfare depicted in epic poetry may not be far removed from the world of the lover after all. Further, *regnat* calls up images of imperial conquest and thus implies that Ovid wants to make an explicit connection between Roman political control and aggression and the amatory practices of the male lover. The *amator*'s cheerful resignation to his new Muse at the conclusion of 1.1 shows that Ovid's lover, paradoxically, seems perfectly satisfied that he has become the booty of *Amor*. The *amator* does not even pretend to be the wretched, unhappy lover expected of a *servus amoris*; he makes evident from the beginning that he is engaged in a deceptive game. As Leslie Cahoon points out, the male lover in 1.1 "delights in being Cupid's victim because he can thereby victimize others."[15] For Ovid's *amator*, *amor* means capture and conquest—all the lover needs to perpetuate his poetic practice is a *praeda*. And although the *amator* proclaims himself to be the *praeda* of his mistress, in *Amores* 1.3 we will see how he merely adopts that pose to conquer and subjugate her.

Although *Amores* 1.3, 1.5, and 1.7 have received significant critical attention, scholars have generally ignored the inscription of gender in the construction of amatory relations in these poems. Indeed, none of the approaches to them attempts to link the lover's mythologizing and "idealization" of his mistress to a particularly masculine point of view.[16] I want to explore, in all three poems, how the positioning of the two sexes clearly privileges the male through the mechanisms of voyeurism and fetishism. Furthermore, I will argue that those mechanisms are male operations because the desire of the male carries agency and power, whereas that of the female does not. As I will show in my discussion of *Amores* 1.5 and 1.7, the objectification of the woman fixed in the position of icon, spectacle, or *image to be looked at* is linked to the sexual pleasure of the narrator enacted through his violent domination and devaluation of his mistress.

As I discussed in the previous chapter, Luce Irigaray ("This Sex Which Is Not One") and Jessica Benjamin (*The Bonds of Love*) critique Freud's accounts of both male and female sexuality. Irigaray's argument that women are turned into statues in the process of specularization has much in common with the theories of feminist film critics about the gendered positions of spectatorship—theories that may be applied fruitfully to Ovid's particular construction of male and female positions within his *amator*'s "narrative."

A number of feminist film theorists have demonstrated how, in cinema, the woman is deprived of a gaze, deprived of subjectivity, and is figured as the object of a masculine scopophilic desire. This construction of the observer as male and the observed as female is articulated lucidly in E. Ann Kaplan's essay "Is the Gaze Male?": "The gaze is not necessarily male (literally) but to own and activate the gaze, given our language and the structure of the unconscious, is to be in the masculine position . . . men do not simply look; their gaze carries with it the power of action and of possession that is lacking in the female gaze" (311, 319). Similarly, in her analysis of the male gaze, the feminist film theorist Mary Ann Doane argues that the hierarchical configuration of observer and observed is one in which "the male is the mover of narrative while the female's association with space or *matter* deprives her of her subjectivity."[17] Teresa de Lauretis also observes that it is the male who "commands at once the action and the landscape" and the female who is assigned the place of object, the recipient of male desire, the passive recipient of his gaze.[18] *Amores* 1.3, 1.5, and 1.7 all demonstrate the ways in which the female's association with *materia*, her position as the fetishized object of the male narrator's gaze, and her identification with her *function* (as "plot-space," "topos") in literary discourse reveal a version of male desire which devalues women and turns them into objects of male fantasies of erotic domination.

Amores 1.3

Katherine Olstein and Leo Curran both offer convincing arguments that *Amores* 1.3 initiates a pattern not only of the *amator*'s deceptive practices toward his mistress but also of his increasingly blatant posturing that allows us to "see through his protestations" of *fides*. Thus, both Olstein and Curran view 1.3 as the first poem in the collection which reveals the inconsistencies and contradictions in the narrator's amatory rhetoric. Moreover, they both argue that these contradictions suggest that Ovid's *amator* is playing a "clearly defined part" and that the mask he wears is that of the typical lover of Roman elegy. Curran's argument about the revelation of the amator's "insincerity" is based on Curran's assertion that the identification of the lover's mistress with the three mythological heroines in the poem identifies, in turn, the narrator with Jupiter; *both* the *amator* and Jupiter are *desultores amoris*. Curran's point is astute, and I believe any interpretation of the poem must take it into account.

Neither Olstein nor Curran, however, considers the implications of their own observations about the *amator*'s duplicitous ways. They both describe the *amator*'s lack of sincerity without any exploration either of what Ovid may be saying about such amatory practices or of the particular gender roles inscribed in what Olstein calls "Ovid's dynamic, topsy-turvy couple game." They point up the wit and playfulness in Ovid's charming conceits, but they fail to identify the couple game as one that involves both male aggression and the blatant figuration of women as both helpless captives and objects of male fantasy and desire.[19]

In 1.3, the first of seven elegies in which the *amator* is identified with Jupiter—who is notorious for ravishing innocent women through a multitude of disguises—Ovid clearly associates amatory relations with the violent subjugation and deception of female "victims." At first glance, Ovid's *amator* in 1.3 appears to adopt the familiar role of the modest, subservient lover whose lack of status is balanced by his poetic talent—a talent, he promises, which will bring to the *puella* the same *fama* accorded the heroines of mythology. But, as Leo Curran has argued, the rhetorical, persuasive aspect of the poem emphasizes the way in which the speaker is playing the clearly defined, conventional role of the lover to achieve the practical end of seducing his mistress. The speaker's stance of modesty about his lowly status and his deferential posture toward the *puella* are thrown into sharp relief when he announces at line 11 that his *comites* are none other than Phoebus himself, along with Bacchus and the Muses. He jumps from one extreme to the other, from excessive self-effacement to boastful claims about his talent.

In addition, that the speaker is wearing a mask and playing at being the elegiac lover becomes clear in his choice of mythological heroines with whom he compares his *puella*. The ostensible reason for including these mythological allusions is to support the speaker's argument about his ability to confer *fama*. Io, Leda, and Europa serve as examples of women who have been immortalized in verse. But the analogy between these three women and the *puella* also suggests a correlation between their lover, Jupiter, and Ovid himself.[20]

The effect of the parallel between the speaker and Jupiter is to undercut the *amator*'s denial of being a *desultor amoris*, a jumper from one woman to another. In addition, the speaker characterized himself earlier as the girl's booty (line 1), but the three women he names are all *praeda* themselves. These contradictions in the speaker's analogy reinforce further the picture of the *amator* as a trickster, moving in and out of various roles and guises to suit his amatory purposes. Furthermore, the parallel between the speaker and Jupiter stresses the violence and dehumanization in the *amator*'s attitudes and practices toward his mistress. Because of Juno's jealousy about his love for Io, Jupiter turns Io into a cow to disguise her. Not only does Jupiter "take" Io but he also robs her of her humanity in the process. In the myths of Europa and

Leda, Jupiter exploits their innocent, unsuspecting natures by using deception to gratify his desires. In like manner, the *amator* poses as a *servus amoris* to persuade his mistress to give herself to him.

The myths he chooses to "win over" his mistress suggest a paradigm for amatory relations which contradicts completely the image of the lover as "enslaved" to the woman. Indeed, the female figures in the myths are all captives of the male, and moreover, their *fama* is at great cost to them. Io got *fama* but at the expense of her humanity and her freedom. Moreover, Io, as a cow, is deprived of language, and thus she is stripped of any ability to lay claim to the status of subject.[21] Without her humanity, without voice, Io is the sexualized object in a narrative constituted by the male poetic voice. That is precisely what the *amator* is offering to his mistress: *fama* in exchange for the loss of her autonomy and humanity.

In addition, the speaker shows that the power and means he has to get what he wants are greater than those of Jupiter himself. The poet, unlike Jupiter, can write about his conquests and the metamorphoses required to make them. Like the eternal relationship between Jupiter and his three heroines, the speaker claims that his mistress will also be his *cura perennis* as a result of their literary union. One may wonder what kind of reward that really is for the woman; *cura* can have the implication of guardianship, and joined with *perennis*, it is possible to see that what the *amator* is offering is not so much eternal devotion as perpetual captivity. This sense of ownership of the woman can only be achieved fully by stripping her of her specificity and humanity. Thus the speaker asks the *puella* to offer herself to him as "fertile material" for his poems: *te mihi materiem felicem in carmina praebe* [Offer yourself to me as fertile material for your songs] (line 19). Here the elegiac woman becomes the site of generation for the male lover. *Te*, in apposition to *materiem felicem*, equates the woman's identity with materiality and thus invokes stereotypical associations of the woman with both a field to be ploughed and a blank surface, "a field not for plowing but for inscription."[22] Calling the *puella* his *materia* turns the woman into a dehumanized commodity, little more than a vehicle for the *amator* to display his talents. Mary-Kay Gamel points out that "in this scheme, the male poet is the farmer/writer, the woman the earth/empty tablet on which he plows/writes."[23] Indeed, the use of the word *felix* in its most literal meaning—to describe the character of the particular *materia* potentially offered by the mistress—emphasizes the woman's use in terms of how she may be fruitful or productive for the male. The more figurative sense of *felix* as *fortunate* or *happy* used in the context of comparing the *puella* with mythological heroines who were victimized by Jupiter becomes highly ironic. The *amator*'s view of his mistress as potential "happy matter" (*materiem felicem*) seems a biased view, at best, and sinister at worst. None of the mythological heroines chosen by the male narrator as a paradigm ends up *felix* at all. On the contrary, they are all helpless victims of male deceit and sexual aggression. More importantly, they are presented exclusively in terms of their *function* as objects of male desire, as fruitful resources to plough for the male lover's erotic and literary advantage.

Amores 1.5

Amores 1.5 presents what is perhaps the most dramatic example of Ovid's depiction of the elegiac mistress as a fetishized object of the narrator's gaze. This is where Corinna first appears as a named figure in the collection, a form "first seen whole."[24] This poem is dramatic in its portrayal of a seemingly explicit and "realistic" erotic encounter between the *amator* and his mistress. Early studies have tended to see the poem either as a "straightforward account of a successful act of love"[25] or as an artful, though shallow, depiction of a sexual romp.[26] More recently, Stephen Hinds and Alison Keith have argued that Corinna's initial appearance in the collection "is effected as a quasi-divine epiphany"[27] with the suggestion of "something supernatural" in the background of the poem. Neither the "realistic" nor the "supernatural" approach, however, accounts for Ovid's strategy of critique in the elegies or for the way gender relations are depicted in the poem. I shall argue that Ovid's poem neither dramatizes an explicit erotic encounter between the *amator* and his mistress nor presents Corinna as a goddess, even an "adumbrated" one.[28] In particular, Hinds' view that *Amores* 1.5 presents Corinna as a form "seen whole" shows an indifference to the fact that Corinna is depicted as anything but whole. On the contrary, she is all parts—dismembered and fragmented by the *amator*'s controlling gaze.

> Aestus erat, mediamque dies exegerat horam;
>   adposui medio membra levanda toro.
> pars adaperta fuit, pars altera clausa fenestrae,
>   quale fere silvae lumen habere solent,
> 5 qualia sublucent fugiente crepuscula Phoebo
>   aut ubi nox abiit nec tamen orta dies.
> illa verecundis lux est praebenda puellis,
>   qua timidus latebras speret habere pudor.
> ecce, Corinna venit tunica velata recincta,
> 10 candida dividua colla tegente coma,

>   qualiter in thalamos formosa Semiramis isse
>   dicitur et multis Lais amata viris.
>   deripui tunicam; nec multum rara nocebat,
>   pugnabat tunica sed tamen illa tegi;
> 15   quae, cum ita pugnaret tamquam quae vincere nollet,
>   victa est non aegre proditione sua.
>   ut stetit ante oculos posito velamine nostros,
>   in toto nusquam corpore menda fuit:
>   quos umeros, quales vidi tetigique lacertos!
> 20   forma papillarum quam fuit apta premi!
>   quam castigato planus sub pectore venter!
>   quantum et quale latus! quam iuvenale femur!
>   singula quid referam? nil non laudabile vidi,
>   et nudam pressi corpus ad usque meum.
> 25   cetera quis nescit? lassi requievimus ambo.
>   proveniant medii sic mihi saepe dies.

[It was hot, and the day had passed its mid hour. I laid my members to rest in the middle of the bed. A part of the window was open, the other part closed. The light came through as it does in a woodland, or as the twilight that glows at sunset, or when night has gone and the day hasn't begun. It was a light for shy girls, where timid modesty might hope for a hiding place. Look! Corinna comes clad in a loose dress, her white neck covered with her parted hair, as, it is said, were the beautiful Semiramis as she went into her bridal-chamber and Lais loved by many men. I tore off her dress; it didn't do much harm it was so scanty. But still she struggled to have the dress cover her. She fought as though she preferred not to win, and she was conquered easily by her own betrayal. As she stood before our eyes with her clothing laid aside, nowhere on her whole body was there a blemish. What shoulders, what arms did I see and touch! How suited for caress was the shape of her breasts! How smooth her belly under her slender bosom! How long and exquisite her flank! How youthful her thigh! Why should I recount every detail? I saw nothing that was not praiseworthy, and I clasped her naked body close to mine. Who doesn't know the rest? Exhausted, we both lay sleeping. May my afternoons often turn out this way!]

The elegy begins with the speaker's description of himself lying languorously in his dimly lit bedroom. Most critics have taken the first word in the poem, *aestus*, to denote weather conditions, and thus they interpret the scene as occurring in the hot summer. But *aestus* can also imply a state of mind. From *aestus* alone we cannot be certain that the speaker means anything *other* than his aroused and titillated mood. This ambiguity is reinforced by his half-full/half-empty window imagery in the opening lines, what Hinds calls "the confusing over-determination of that half-light."[29] The chiaroscuro effect of the window image suggests perceptual ambiguity. Indeed, there is an artificiality in the way everything seems perfectly and symmetrically arranged. The excessive symmetry with which the speaker describes the scene, *mediamque . . . medio membra . . . pars . . . pars,* further suggests that the speaker's experience of the setting is a projection of his own erotic imagination.

The half-light of the speaker's bedroom, like the obscurely lit woodland in line 4, does not, as Hinds argues, hint at divine epiphany but rather the perceptual dimness that animates the speaker's imagination. There is no evidence of divine presence here. The similes that follow the narrator's description of the scene, in lines 4–6, emphasize his engagement with his own active imagination and its ability to construct its own interpretation of reality. The obscure light is seen alternatively as that of dawn *and* as that of dusk.

Although woods are a common setting for divine apparitions in Roman poetry,[30] here the woodland setting is presented in conjunction with the twilight images that stress a flexibility of interpretation and perception. W. S. M. Nicoll suggests that the speaker's allusion to *silvae* has a "decidedly Vergilian character."[31] I would argue, however, that Ovid's narrator asserts a resistance to epic and does so not merely by replacing divine apparitions with the appearance of *puellae* but by contradicting expectations of the divine with the emphasis on his own private perceptual fantasies. In the *Aeneid,* apparitions occur either in a context in which the hero is reminded or made aware of his destiny in the cosmic order or when his unconscious drives or emotions rise to the surface in a personified form.[32] In Ovid's poem, the male lover is not spurred by outside forces to participate in heroic action. More importantly, the *amator* appears highly conscious of his ability to control and manipulate the ways in which his world may be arranged and perceived. At lines 7–8, the *amator* prepares us for the sudden "appearance" of his mistress by describing yet another way the dim light of his bedroom may be construed: as *illa verecundis lux est praebenda puellis.*

The apparent abruptness of Corinna's "arrival" at line 9 leads critics with the "realistic" approach to assume either that the narrator simply was not expecting visitors or that he had arranged the lighting with seduction in mind.[33] But the *amator* does not arrange the lighting; he only describes different ways it may be viewed. He does not *do* anything to alter the setting. Rather, the *amator* constructs a vivid set of pictures which conveys his absorption in his own image making. Those who take the "supernatural" approach, on the other hand, read the narrator's exclamatory announcement of Corinna's seemingly unanticipated appearance—*ecce, Corinna venit*—as suggestive of a divine apparition. Thus Hinds remarks, "Another circumstantial hint may be felt in the *manner* of Corinna's arrival. No knock at the door, no explanation of her sudden presence, half-clothed (*tunica velata recincta*), in Ovid's chamber: just (1.5.9) *ecce, Corinna venit*. Is this simple narrative economy—or a hint also of dream-like epiphany?"[34] Hinds is right in suggesting that Corinna's appearance has more to do with the narrator's own powers of imagination than with the presence of an actual mistress. But the narrator, as we will see, hardly presents Corinna in terms befitting a goddess. In addition, whether Corinna is actually in the room with the speaker or not is immaterial. She is like the light in the room; it is there, but its specific nature is fluid and is described by a grammatically constant *ego* whose perceptions and desires define the nature of what it sees.

As in the case of the partly open, partly closed window and the light that is either at dawn or dusk, Corinna too is presented in binary terms. On the one hand, she is clad in a loosened or ungirded tunic (*venit tunica velata recincta*); on the other hand, the *amator* speaks of her fair neck covered with her neatly parted hair (*candida dividua colla tegente coma*). In the first instance, Corinna appears to be ready for an erotic encounter; her loosened dress suggests a laxity of virtue. In the second view, the *amator* directs our attention to the part in Corinna's hair as if to suggest her modesty and restraint. The similes that follow these descriptions of Corinna reinforce the speaker's ambiguous presentation of her *qualiter in thalamos formosa Semiramis isse / dicitur et multis Lais amata viris* [as it is said were the beautiful Semiramis as she entered her bridal-chambers and Lais loved by many men]. In the first simile, the narrator evokes a virgin bride entering her bridal chamber. Thus this image seems to echo the earlier image of Corinna as a *timida puella* hiding in the shadows. But in fact Semiramis was notorious not only as the powerful legendary queen of Babylon but as a woman known for her sexual prowess.[35] Indeed, even in Ovid's version, there is a touch of sarcasm; Semiramis enters not one bridal chamber, but many or, at least more than one (*thalamos*).[36] Juvenal's reference to Semiramis (2.128) emphasizes her association with the East and with Cleopatra. According to Diodorus, Semiramis was known as a woman who embodied "masculine" daring, not only in her capacity as a ruler but also in her epic abilities to subjugate others to her will.[37] From an Augustan perspective, Semiramis may well have been identified with moral degeneracy and unbridled female lust—or at least with the transgression of social norms for women. Thus, picturing Corinna as *both* chaste bride and wanton woman in the figure of Semiramis is perhaps the ultimate sexual turn-on for the male lover in the poem. He clearly derives the greatest pleasure from conjuring images of his mistress which run the gamut from *verecunda puella* (shy girl) in line 7, to a powerful and sexually active queen, to the courtesan of Corinth in line 12—an object of exchange and desire in the sexual marketplace. Ovid extends the stereotype of the woman as either virgin or whore by having his *amator* describe his desired woman as a paradigm of *both* virtue and licentiousness. In addition, the movement in the poem from modest *puella* to wanton prostitute may be correlated with a heightening of sexual desire in the *amator*, as suggested by his blunt announcement in line 13, *deripui tunicam* [I tore off her dress].

The language and atmosphere shift from the sultry languorousness in the first half of the poem to an impression of heightened realism. Once the speaker's desires are aroused by both the sight of his mistress and his fantasies of her as queen and courtesan, the amatory scene becomes one of struggle and conquest. In lines 13–15, the *amator* describes the erotic encounter in terms of domination and conquest; the repetition of the verb *pugnare* emphasizes the extent to which the speaker frames amatory experience as a kind of military conquest. Not only does the speaker describe his mistress as the loser in the battle of love (*victa est*) but he presumes that her efforts to fight him off are merely a charade to arouse him further. Imagining her resistance at the same time that she desires him "deep down" allows the *amator* to picture his mistress in a way that best serves and mirrors his own desires—and picture her he does.

The description of Corinna's naked body in lines 17–22 is generally seen by critics as "one of the fullest portraits of a mistress in Latin elegy";[38] it is a portrait that displays Corinna's "magnificent stature" and "the attributes of an idealised mistress . . . the attributes of a goddess."[39] But it is difficult to see how the speaker's presentation of his mistress's body as merely a composite of details—a series of dismembered images—can be regarded as either "magnificent" or godlike.[40] At line 17, the speaker begins by declaring that Corinna stood naked before his eyes. The inertness of the image of Corinna standing, expressed by the phrase *ut stetit* [thus she stood], suggests a statuelike quality that reinforces the earlier view of her as a projection of the speaker's fantasies and desires. Indeed, Keith has observed that Corinna's body here "displays a perfection realizable only in a work of art such as a marble statue, an ivory carving, or a finely crafted book of poetry."[41] The speaker's Corinna completely lacks blemish: *in toto nusquam corpore menda fuit* (18). As Keith points out, the word *menda* is used frequently as a metaphor to connote literary faults. Thus Keith argues that the *amator* "implicitly conflates" the *corpus* of his mistress and his literary *corpus*. Although this argument draws attention to the figure of Corinna as a literary construction, it fails to consider the degree to which the *amator*'s dismembering portrayal of the woman presents the female body in the context of what Peter Green calls a "successful act of love."[42]

The emphasis on the eyes (*oculos nostros*) of the male observer—along with his particularizing mode of figuring the body—focuses attention on how Corinna is a spectacle, the fixed object of the *amator*'s ravishing gaze. Or, in Nancy Vickers' terms, she is a body fetishized by a poetic voice in a process that entails an obsessive dismembering of the female body, an insistence on describing the woman through the isolation of her parts. In this context, Laura Mulvey's analysis of the gaze in film narrative seems useful in approaching the way Ovid portrays the relationship between the male narrator and the aestheticized female.[43] Mulvey's discussion of women in Hollywood cinema, in particular through her reference to Freud's theories about scopophilia (pleasure in looking), can shed light on the figure of Corinna in *Amores* 1.5. Freud, Mulvey points out, associated scopophilia with objectifying others and subjecting them to a "controlling and curious gaze." Scopophilia involves using another person as an object of sexual arousal through the mechanism of sight. In cinema, women have traditionally played an exhibitionist role, as signifiers of male desire. In Mulvey's words, "The determining male gaze projects its fantasy onto the female figure, which is styled accordingly."[44] Thus, the *woman as spectacle* is both a mirror for male desire and a source of arousal. Moreover, conventional close-ups of women in film tend to isolate particular parts of their bodies. The fragmented body thus destroys the illusion of depth and gives what Mulvey calls "flatness, the quality of a cut-out or icon" to the figuration of the woman's body. The narrator's obsessively particularizing mode of describing Corinna's body in *Amores* 1.5 may thus constitute an analogue to the film close-up. Corinna is displayed as icon, passive and inert, while the male narrator emerges as the representative of power. As the "bearer of the look" the *amator* is free to construct both image and narrative in a three-dimensional space in which *he* defines both the desired sexual object and the narrative area.

Vickers reminds us that the female body fetishized by the male poet allows *his* voice to emerge while the woman's speech is silenced. The fragmentation of Corinna's body seems to constitute the *amator*'s own *corpus*. Her whole body is less than the sum of her parts. In clinical anatomical detail, the speaker enumerates but never unifies each of Corinna's parts—her shoulders, arms, breasts, belly, flank, and thigh. Nowhere in his description of her does the narrator mention Corinna's head, face, or eyes—parts of the body which are most associated with a person's humanity.[45] The *amator* thus dehumanizes his mistress not only through his dismemberment of her but also through a kind of decapitation that renders her lifeless. Without a head, she can neither see nor speak.

Whereas the *amator* is the subject of seeing (*vidi*), Corinna's parts are passive objects of the narrator's touch. Her breasts are *to be caressed*, her shoulders and arms *to be touched*—they exist only for his pleasure, as part of *his* text, his *corpus*. The unity of the speaker's position as subject is constant; at line 23 he emphasizes his own status as both signifier and seer (*singula quid referam? nil non laudabile vidi*). Here the close association of seeing (*vidi*) and speaking (*referam*) is made clear. As possessor of the gaze, the male speaker gathers up the scattered parts of Corinna's body; they are enfolded within his text and collected as *singula* for his remembering. Indeed, her body becomes *corpus* only after it is assimilated to the body of the speaker. Although *pressi* in line 24 is often translated as *I clasped*, it can carry the meaning of *pressing* or *imprinting*. Thus Ovid conveys implicitly the sense that Corinna's body becomes whole (a *corpus* at all) when it is imprinted in the text or *corpus* of the speaker. As a part of the *amator*'s *corpus*, Corinna's voice is subsumed in the *we* of *requievimus*. Subject and object of desire merge as the *amator* speaks both for himself and for Corinna: *lassi requievimus ambo*. In the last line, the speaker's wish that many of his afternoons turn out so well for him (*mihi*) suggests a return to the earlier scene—of the *amator* lying alone in his room. Unlike the "scattered woman" of his fantasies, the *amator*, perhaps *through* the process of dismembering and remembering the female body, remains an integrated subject, unharmed by the struggles (*pugnae*) of amatory experience. As Vickers writes, "If the speaker's 'self' [his text, his *corpus*] is to be unified, it would seem to require the repetition of her dismembered image."[46]

Ovid's poem presents a stark contrast to the Sapphic tradition of portraying amatory experience as both disabling and disintegrating to the lover. In Sappho's famous *phainetai moi* poem, it is the female subject of desire who undergoes a kind of fragmentation as a result of gazing at the beloved,[47] and in numerous translations and imitations of Sappho's poem through the ages male poets have assumed the Sapphic voice and identified themselves with the experience of erotic fragmentation.[48] Indeed, the linkage of seeing and bodily disintegration occupies a central place in the amatory tradition. But, as Lawrence Lipking suggests, erotic fragmentation—that is, bodily and emotional disintegration through visual contact with the beloved—has been associated typically with the feminine. As we saw in the discussion of Catullus' erotic fragmentation in Chapter 1, when the male lover declares that he is victimized by love he becomes feminized. Ovid's *amator*, however, appears to be immune to the shattering effects of *amor* on the self; he approaches his object of desire without the usual rhetoric of amatory passivity and powerlessness. The possessive, controlling gaze is linked unequivocally in Ovid's poem with a male/viewer, female/object exchange and is shown to be the instrument through which the male narrator attains unity at the expense of his mistress's dispersion. With its vivid portrayal of the dismembered woman, *Amores* 1.5 not only presents a rigidly hierarchical view of amatory relations, it also highlights a stark reality of woman's place in the circulation and representation of desire. Whereas the poems of both Sappho and Catullus show the ways in which the gaze "opens the self to disintegration,"[49] Ovid's poems reveal how the operations of the (male) gaze may indeed constitute a transgressive violation of the other.[50] It is no wonder that many critics have failed to see the violence implicit in Ovid's seemingly charming and harmless description of erotic pleasure and the woman who arouses it.[51]

Amores 1.7

In 1.7, the speaker's cavalier attitude about assaulting his mistress and his use of the event as an opportunity for an extravagant display of his poetic talents not only expose the *amator*'s sanctioning of violence in amatory affairs but also show the pleasure and self-enhancement he derives from subjugating his mistress. The speaker carries us on a very bumpy ride of jolting reversals in tone and sensibility as he describes his "remorse" over hitting his mistress.

> Adde manus in vincla meas (meruere catenas)
>   dum furor omnis abit, si quis amicus ades
> nam furor in dominam temeraria bracchia movit;
>   flet mea vesana laesa puella manu.

> [If any friend of mine is here, then tie up my hands (they deserve shackles) until this frenzy has completely gone. For madness caused my rash hands to assault my mistress. She is in tears, injured by my crazy hand.] (lines 1–4)

Although earlier scholars such as Hermann Fränkel, Georg Luck, and L. P. Wilkinson[52] read 1.7 as a serious and sincere expression of Ovid's regret and remorse, more recent scholars have been inclined to emphasize the poem's witty playfulness and its parodic qualities. Both Peter Connor and Douglass

Parker[53] point out how the last two lines of the poem overturn the entire structure, and they make clear that Ovid has been fooling us all along with his protestations of regret. Although I acknowledge that the last distich signals an important reversal in sensibility, I do not agree with Connor that we accept the seriousness of what the speaker says in the rest of the poem. I believe that throughout the entire poem, Ovid takes us through a series of elaborate reversals and transformations of mood, perspective, and poetic style which reflects the ambiguous and contradictory nature of his protagonist. In addition, neither Connor nor Parker considers the satirical aspects of the poem. They merely point out that by the end of the poem, we realize that the speaker's expression of remorse is not genuine. But by showing the *amator* openly trivializing his assault on his mistress—even reveling in it—Ovid implicitly criticizes the moral indifference inherent in such a casual legitimization of violence and exploitation in amatory relations.

The speaker begins by telling anyone who will listen (*si quis amicus ades*, line 2) that he is horrified at having hit his mistress. But his exaggerated expressions of remorse raise suspicions about the genuineness of his emotions. The speaker's use of *furor* in line 3 and *vesana*[54] in line 4 seems out of place and overblown in the context of a personal domestic dispute. Both words are normally associated with a situation of more serious magnitude, frequently with potentially tragic consequence. The incongruity between the extremity of the speaker's language and the actual situation not only creates a comic effect but also trivializes the incident by making it seem petty in contrast to the exaggerated rhetoric used to describe it. This is evident also in the melodramatic way the speaker invokes the most sacrilegious acts imaginable to describe the "seriousness" of his brutality toward the *puella:* violence directed toward both parents and gods: *tunc ego vel caros potui violare parentes / saeva vel in sanctos verbera ferre deos* [I was so mad that I could have harmed my dear parents, or whipped the blessed gods] (lines 5 and 6).

Moreover, the fact that the speaker does not blame himself but rather his hands and arms raises further doubts about how remorseful he really is. Describing his rage in terms that make him sound like a criminal is supposed to be an unequivocal admission of culpability. However, the speaker's equivocation and inconsistency begin to show through when he cites mythological precedents for his behavior. On the one hand, he urges his friends to enchain him, but then, on the other, he tries to minimize his responsibility by saying that even two of the most renowned heroes in myth, Ajax and Orestes, succumbed to *furor:*

> quid? non et clipei dominus septemplicis Ajax
>   stravit deprensos lata per arva greges,
> et vindex in matre patris, malus ultor, Orestes
>   ausus in arcanas poscere tela deas?
> ergo ego digestos potui laniare capillos?
>   nec dominam motae dedecuere comae:
> sic formosa fuit

[Why? Didn't seven-shielded Ajax go berserk through the meadows, slaughtering sheep, and didn't Orestes, the evil avenger, the defender of his father against his mother, dare to call for weapons against the Furies? Therefore, was I able to tear her arranged coiffure? Her hair all in disarray looked beautiful.] (lines 7–13)

Not only does the speaker make the assault on his mistress seem trivial, but he also remarks that she actually looks more beautiful to him as a result of what he has done to her. Curran points out a parallel situation in the *Metamorphoses:* "Beauty and desirability are enhanced by disarray of clothing or hair, by discomfort or embarrassment, or by fear. For the rapist these are all aphrodisiacs. Daphne's hair and dress are attractively disordered by the breezes as she flees Apollo, and Leucothoe's 'terror was becoming to her'" (*Metamorphoses* 4.230).[55] The *amator* here is clearly titillated by his mistress's dishevelled appearance and by her position as helpless victim. This suggests that the *amator* derives pleasure through control and domination and that the perception of her as beautiful, to some degree, depends on his ability to disparage her.

The speaker's lyrical reverie comparing Corinna's beauty with that of Atalanta, Ariadne, and Cassandra reinforces the linkage in the poem between male sexual desire and domination over the mistress.

>   talem Schoeneida dicam
> Maenalias arcu sollicitasse feras;
>   talis periuri promissaque velaque Thesei
> flevit praecipites Cressa tulisse Notos;
>   sic, nisi vittatis quod erat, Cassandra, capillis,
> procubuit templo, casta Minerva, tuo.

[like Atalanta's while hunting game on the Arcadian hills, or like Ariadne's, when she cried for false Theseus, his promises and his sails borne on the south wind; thus was Cassandra, except for her hair in a fillet, when she knelt at your temple, chaste Minerva.] (lines 13–18)

These mythological *exempla* support the speaker's sanctioning of violence toward his mistress and the pleasure it brings. The implication is that although these women were abused and abandoned by men, it is all worth it because they are "seen" as beautiful objects of desire, and, on top of that, they receive *fama* as a result of their liaisons with men who abuse and/or degrade them. Although Atalanta is pictured here as a huntress, in the myth she is exposed at infancy because her father wants a male heir. Moreover, despite Atalanta's determination to remain independent of men and retain her virginity, she is manipulated by both her father and her bridegroom to give that up. Perhaps there is some suggestion in Ovid's poem that the mistress ought to give up her tears and, like Atalanta, defer to the superior judgment (if not power) of the male. Ariadne's case reinforces more directly the speaker's justification for his violent and demeaning behavior toward his mistress; she was used by Theseus to gain fame and was then abandoned mercilessly on an island. Likewise, Cassandra, according to many accounts, was persecuted by Apollo (he made sure her prophecies would never be believed) because she would not give in to his amorous advances. In addition, some accounts say Cassandra was a victim of rape as well, and then she was "taken" against her will by Agamemnon and killed by Clytemnestra merely because of Agamemnon's folly in bringing her home as his concubine. The speaker uses these examples to prove or justify the beauty of his mistress by raising her to mythological status. But doing so distances Corinna, as a real person, from him. Furthermore, Corinna is most desirable to the *amator* when she is made part of a mythological schema in which women are figured as helpless, captive victims. The *amator* in 1.7 justifies violence toward his mistress by creating "beautiful" images of defenseless women who are rescued and subjugated by men.

In lines 31–34, the parallel the speaker draws between the incident in the *Iliad* in which Diomedes strikes Aphrodite and his own assault on the *puella* has an ambiguous effect.

> pessima Tydides scelerum monimenta reliquit:
>   ille deam primus perculit; alter ego.
> et minus ille nocens: mihi quam profitebar amare
>   laesa est; Tydides saevus in hoste fuit.

[Diomedes left behind the worst memorial of wicked deeds; he was the first to strike a goddess, I was next. He was less guilty. I hurt the one I professed to love, Diomedes was savage against an enemy.]

On the surface, the example of Diomedes expresses the speaker's guilt because he admits that what he did was worse: he hit the woman he loved, whereas Diomedes struck his enemy. But the highly rhetorical aspect of comparing himself with Diomedes in the hope that his mistress will forgive him suggests that he is striking a pose. Self-conscious flattery of the *puella* is implied in the way the speaker exploits the elegiac cliché of turning the mistress into a goddess. The analogy that correlates the speaker with Diomedes also indicates that the woman is analogous to Venus herself. But if the speaker had sincerely wished to flatter his mistress, he could have chosen a better moment in Venus' mythological history. The example he does choose emphasizes her humiliation and defeat at the hands of a great military hero. When the speaker gets carried away with his image of the mistress as his captive, it reinforces the connection in the poem between pleasure and male domination.

> i nunc, magnificos victor molire triumphos,
>   cinge comam lauro votaque redde Iovi,
> quaeque tuos currus comitantem turba sequetur,
>   clamet 'io, forti victa puella viro est!'
> ante eat effuso tristis captive capillo,
>   si sinerent laesae, candida tota, genae.
> aptius impressis fuerat livere labellis
>   et collum blandi dentis habere notam.
>
> [Go now, victor, in magnificent triumph, wreathe your hair with laurel, render thanks to Jove, and let the crowd follow your chariot, and shout, "hail, brave man who defeated a girl!" Let her walk ahead, a captive, hair all dishevelled, completely pale, except for the scratches on her cheeks. Bruised lips, bites on the neck and shoulders would have been more appropriate scars.] (lines 35–42)

The scars of love, bruised lips and bites on the neck, sound curiously similar to the scratches on the girl's cheeks. The link between the two also undercuts the speaker's claims of guilt because demonstrations of affection appear to be so close to physical abuse. But, at line 51, the speaker shifts his attention from his "brutish" behavior toward his mistress to an image of her as a trembling victim who evokes sympathy and compassion. The speaker, however, undercuts this apparent genuineness of sympathy for his mistress by delighting in his own artistry. His series of five similes to describe her terror has the effect of removing the reader from the narrative situation as well as suggesting the speaker's emotional distance from the suffering of his mistress.

She becomes a pictorial object in the speaker's imaginative landscape, the "empty tablet" on which the *amator* can inscribe his poetic talents. The *amator* metaphorizes the woman right out of sentient existence and again diverts attention from his violent behavior to his poetic virtuosity. His pose of remorse is overshadowed by the way he seems to relish the opportunity this violent incident affords him to dazzle his audience with a stunning display of his genius. Brutality toward the woman is rationalized through the *amator*'s transformation of his mistress into inanimate objects. She ceases to be a woman—a victim of male aggression—and becomes a series of items in a benign natural landscape.

> astitit illa amens albo et sine sanguine vultu,
>   caeduntur Pariis qualia saxa iugis;
> exanimis artus et membra trementia vidi,
>   ut cum populeas ventilat aura comas,
> ut leni Zephyro gracilis vibratur harundo
>   summave cum tepido stringitur unda Noto

[She stood there bewildered, her face pale and bloodless, as new-hewn Parian marble. I saw her lifeless body and her limbs trembling, as when a breeze blows through poplar leaves, or when the graceful reed quivers from the light wind, or when the top of the wave is ruffled by the warm breeze.] (lines 51–56)

The first simile compares the frightened woman to blocks of white Parian marble. The image of Parian marble recalls the ivory statue of Pygmalion and suggests that, like Pygmalion, Ovid's *amator* sees his elegiac mistress here as an art-object—inanimate and voiceless. Indeed, the parallel between Pygmalion and the *amator* also suggests that, like Pygmalion, the *amator* too falls in love with his own creation.[56] Further, *vidi*, in line 53, clearly positions the male narrator as a *spectator* as well as "creator and lover of his art-object,"[57] while the woman occupies the position as the passive recipient of the speaker's regulatory gaze. As de Lauretis puts it, "female is what is not susceptible to transformation, to life or death; she (it) is an element of plot-space, a topos . . . matrix and matter" (43–44).[58] Indeed, the male narrator in 1.7 has turned his mistress into an "it," into his poetic *materia*, an immobile feature of *his* plot-space.

The next four similes compare the woman to objects in nature: poplar leaves, the slender reed, the surface of a wave, and water distilled from snow. In these four similes, the objects in nature are not only inanimate but are all subject to a more powerful force in nature which controls their movement. The woman is thus rendered doubly powerless by the male narrator who pictures her as both *amens* and as lacking in agency of her own. At line 61, the image of the speaker kneeling before his mistress and trying unsuccessfully three times to clasp her feet is meant to stress his guilt and his fear of losing her.

> ter tamen ante pedes volui procumbere supplex;
>   ter formidatas reppulit illa manus.
> at tu ne dubita (minuet vindicta dolorem)
>   protinus in voltus unguibus ire meos;
> nec nostris oculis nec nostris parce capillis:
>   quamlibet infirmas adiuvat ira manus.
> neve mei sceleris tam tristia signa supersint,
>   pone recompositas in statione comas.

[Nevertheless, three times I wanted to kneel at her feet in supplication. Three times she thrust off those dreadful hands. Don't hesitate (revenge lessens the pain) to vent your anger against my face with your nails. Spare neither my eyes nor my hair: anger helps weak hands. And that you do not remove the sad signs of my crime, rearrange your hair the way it was.] (lines 61–68)

But the sudden shift from the tender scene of supplication to the speaker's brash incitement to violence reveals that his expressions of remorse are adopted only for effect. In many of his elegies, the narrator reveals that he is shamelessly willing to say whatever he feels is necessary to get his way and that if one strategy does not work, he—very often abruptly—changes his tone and his tactics accordingly. Here, when the speaker's efforts to persuade his mistress fail, he quickly drops his lofty rhetoric and tries a different approach. In the final analysis, the speaker abandons all pretenses of remorse by no longer hiding his casual acceptance of violence and domination behind a mask of literary rhetoric and mythological allusion.

That the speaker drops his mask is reinforced by his shift from a third-person narrative to second-person address. For the first time in the poem, the speaker apostrophizes his mistress directly. His first words to her, however, not only sanction violence but actually invite his mistress to retaliate against his assault by being as brutal toward him as she likes. Although he encourages his mistress to use violence, the tone of that encouragement suggests that he does not really fear she will do so. Furthermore, the use of imperatives (*dubita, parce, pone*) in his message to her emphasizes the *amator*'s continued domination and control over her. H. Akbar Khan suggests that it is possible to read *infirmas . . . manus* in a military sense, to mean "troops who are not powerful," and thus Khan proposes that "we can with ease imagine a general on the field of battle exhorting his sparse troops to make up by their indignation for a deficit in numbers."[59] Khan, however, regards this military allusion as merely a clever conceit on Ovid's part. The image of the *amata* as a general leading troops that are *infirmas* seems highly ironic in light of the earlier images of the mistress as an inanimate block of marble. Moreover, we can see in the last line of the poem when the *amator* tells his mistress to put her hair *in statione* that it is the male lover rather than his mistress who is most closely associated with the role of a general ordering his troops to assume their proper rank.

In the last two lines of the poem, the *amator* shows a callousness toward his mistress and an overall moral indifference when he implies that he wants her to take the assault in stride and simply resume the relationship as though nothing had ever happened. Commanding his mistress to put her hair *in statione* not only trivializes the whole incident but also shows the *amator*'s binary views of his mistress. Earlier in the poem, the *amator* was clearly titillated by the mistress' disarray (brought on by his violent behavior) and showed how the consequences of his assault of her fueled his creative imagination as well. But at the end of the poem, the *amator*'s insistence that his mistress rein in her disordered locks and assume her proper *statio* (in its double connotations of "social station" and military rank) invokes both social and political hierarchies. Moreover, it suggests a desire to constrain female sexuality and subjugate the woman to the watchful guardianship of the male. By telling his mistress to remove the *signa* of his misdeed, the male narrator assumes supreme control and becomes the sole signifier, the sole maker of meanings, of how things will be seen and understood. As the *tabula rasa* that lacks both form and rationality (*amens*), the woman in Ovid's elegies owes her existence, her *nomen*, to the male whose gaze renders her as spectacle, as *matter* for literary discourse, while she herself remains outside the processes of signification.

Olstein, Curran, Khan, and others have insisted that the *Amores* demonstrate "with perennially enduring wit, how the game of love works." But their analyses fail to recognize a crucial dimension in Ovid's presentation of love. Ovid does indeed show us how the game works, but he does so by revealing how the elegiac stance of servitude toward the mistress is often self-serving for the *amator* and dehumanizing toward women. Ovid shows how the game is, very often, no happy matter (*felix materia*) for women. Furthermore, Ovid's portrayal of amatory relations displays both men and women caught in the mechanisms of power and domination, mechanisms that, to be sure, privilege the male but may indeed provoke us to wonder if men, as well as women, are prisoners of gender in the game of love.

CHAPTER FIVE

Sexual Politics in Ovid's *Amores*

*I*n Chapter 4 we saw how the poems in Book 1 of the *Amores* expose the destructive aspects of *amor* by revealing a pattern of gender relations which revolves around the portrayal of the elegiac mistress as a commodified object. In this chapter we shall expand our investigation of Ovid's critique of *amor* by examining poems in Books 2 and 3. I will argue that the *amator*'s blatant deception and exploitation of women demonstrate how the version of *amor* practiced by the *amator* is woven inextricably with an ideology of male domination and power which reflects Roman mercantilist and imperialist attitudes. Indeed, Ovid's arrangement of the poems in the *Amores* shows his narrator's increasing pessimism about amatory relations. The *amator* seems, at first, to adopt the conventional role of the elegiac lover and gradually reveals that his persona as a *servus amoris* is a posture "we are invited to penetrate."[1] But the later poems in the collection paint a more blatant picture of the *amator*'s use of deception to get what he wants and an increasing indifference to the moral implications of his amatory attitudes and practices. Unlike his poetic predecessors, for Ovid the world of *amor* and the world of the marketplace are, by no means, so different from one another.[2] In earlier poems in the *Amores*, Ovid shows how deception is an effective strategy for attaining the *amator*'s desires. But in a number of the poems in the second and third books — particularly those that show open adultery in which women are treated as commodities of exchange between their husbands and their lovers—Ovid presents a view of Roman society which sanctions exploitation and brutality toward women.

The flagrant indifference of the *amator* to the moral implications of his amatory practices conveys Ovid's attempt to destroy the myth of the elegiac lover as the upholder of an ideal that is morally superior to the conventional values of Roman society. As Julie Hemker observes, in Ovid's version of the rape of the Sabine women in the *Ars Amatoria*, Ovid calls into question the legitimacy of the men's actions by focusing sympathetically on the helplessness of the women and the horror of their situation.[3] Hemker also observes that in the early books of the *Metamorphoses*, Ovid relates the inner terror of sexually abused virgins. Ovid's sympathetic portrayal of women who are victimized by predatory males in the *Metamorphoses* can be linked to a somewhat unsympathetic portrayal of the lover in the *Amores*, a lover whose selfish attempts to gratify his own desires, no matter what the cost to his victims, may also be regarded as predatory and exploitative. In the *Amores*, however, Ovid does not explore the responses of the *amator*'s female victims. Instead, Ovid offers only the *amator*'s perspective, which, as Mary-Kay Gamel has argued, "is conspicuously marked as male."[4] The blasé, facile way the *amator* manipulates, deceives, and uses others for his own erotic advantage forces us to see, if not condemn, the uglier, less idealized, less romanticized side of amatory experience. Superficially, the *Amores* seems to endorse "duplicity as a way of love,"[5] but on a deeper level I believe Ovid is criticizing not only the hypocrisy of the whole elegiac model with its attendant romantic illusions, but more importantly, the cruel, destructive, and inhumane aspects of *amor*.

In this chapter I shall argue that Ovid extends his critique of violence and exploitation of women to a more general critique of a social and political system that promotes aggression, conquest, and the exploitation of others. My discussion will focus on poems in the second and third books which show most clearly not only the *amator*'s unabashedly deceitful manner but also how Ovid attempts to expose and ridicule the hypocrisy that is inherent in the elegiac ideal—an ideal based on the illusion of *fides*. Further, I will show, particularly in poems in the third book, that Ovid exposes not only the cynical mercantilism in his narrator's amatory attitudes and practices but also how the hegemonic discourse of the *amator* is connected with the colonizing and patriarchal value system that had existed in Rome for centuries.

Indeed, Ovid's use of military metaphors to describe amatory experience takes on greater force in the second and third books. The *amator*'s increasingly explicit identification with masculine aggression and military conquest as his mode of conduct and discourse in amatory affairs points up essential linkages between the Roman public world and private consciousness. Ovid suggests that sexual violence and the exploitation of women are paradigmatic of a corrupt social and political system. In tracing the connections between love and conquest in the *Amores,* Leslie Cahoon argues that "the *libido dominandi* deplored by Sallust (*Catullus* 2.2) becomes in the *Amores* a kind of internal moral rot pervading the lives and loves of individuals." Further, Cahoon points out that "by weaving together the vocabularies of love and war, the *Amores* suggest that the ambition to conquer is in the process of destroying *socialia iura.*"[6] Cahoon's argument that Ovid's use of military imagery in the *Amores* constitutes not merely a witty exercise but a serious critique of Roman *amor* opens up significant inquiry into the implications of an isomorphism between sexual and social relations in Ovid's amatory texts.[7]

My own analysis focuses not so much on the theme of erotic warfare but rather on the ways *amor* reiterates values (and practices) of commercialism and imperialist aggression which turn those who are without real power into commodities of exchange. Thus, I argue that in the *Amores* Ovid presents amatory arrangements as transactions that consolidate masculine authority and privilege and reinforce the integration of male sexual and social dominance. In terms articulated by Teresa de Lauretis and a number of other feminist theorists, Ovid presents us with a "sexual politics" rooted in a sex-gender system where sex is correlated to social values and hierarchies that are necessarily interconnected with political and economic conditions.[8] My argument will draw on Gayle Rubin's pioneering analysis of how sex-gender systems are part of a "systematic social apparatus which takes up females as raw materials and fashions domesticated women as products."[9] Rubin's discussion of Claude Lévi-Strauss's view that kinship systems rely primarily on the exchange of women among men will prove especially useful in examining Ovid's portrayal of amatory relations as well. Ovid's amatory texts show us that the private, domestic sphere of sexuality, the family, and affectivity is not a separate domain of existence but a position within social and political realities in general.[10]

Amores 2.11

As we saw in Chapter 4, Ovid's *amator* openly employs deception and exploitation of others to get what he wants. But as I suggested earlier, I do not believe that Ovid is endorsing an approach to love which is based on duplicity and conquest. I think that his purpose is to expose what he considers to be the harsh realities behind the elegiac mask. By so doing, Ovid uncovers the predatory and violent aspects of *amor*. Although at times the reader may admire the *amator* for his clever manipulative abilities, Ovid makes his readers acutely aware of the immorality of his *amator* by portraying his behavior as unabashedly deceitful and exploitative in the extreme. The shockingly facile way the *amator* accepts and even embraces duplicity and violence as inevitable aspects of love suggests that Ovid wants to provoke a sense of outrage in his audience.

In a number of his elegies, Ovid's *amator* says openly that he prefers deception over honesty and at times even asks to be lied to rather than to hear unpleasant truths. *Amores* 2.11, Ovid's version of the convention of the *propemptikon,* is a case in point. On the surface, the speaker in 2.11 is trying to convince his mistress not to depart on her impending journey. In the interest of dissuading Corinna from her voyage, the speaker warns her about the possible dangers she might encounter. But, rather than pleading with her in a tone of anguish, as Propertius does with Cynthia in his *propemptikon*, the speaker describes at great length, with gusto and vivid detail, why a journey by sea would be extremely perilous. Here the *amator* seems to take pleasure in enumerating the various obstacles standing in the way of his progress with the *puella*.[11] Such obstacles make love interesting and challenging to the lover and offer him endless possibilities to strike poses and develop clever maneuvers to overcome whatever stands between him and his beloved.

In his discussion of the poem, Kenneth Quinn argues that the *amator*'s Don Juan persona, with his blasé, flippant attitude, is at odds with the state of mind which is appropriate for an address to a departing mistress.[12] Quinn reads the incongruity as evidence that Ovid is overturning any pretension to seriousness about love because of his speaker's lack of emotional involvement with the amatory situation. But I think Quinn misses part of the point. The speaker's attitude and his romantic posturing in the poem show that he uses Corinna's departure as an opportunity for him to engage in ingenious flights of imagination as he contemplates the adventures she might encounter on her journey. More importantly, that the speaker seems to look forward to the opportunity to hear Corinna's fictions about her journey when she returns suggests that Ovid is quite serious about showing how deception is often both inevitable and necessary to maintain amatory relations.

The poem begins with an overblown, incongruous comparison between the lover's misfortunes and those of epic and tragic heroes:

>Prima malas docuit mirantibus aequoris undis
>   Peliaco pinus vertice caesa vias,
>quae concurrentis inter temeraria cautes

> conspicuam fuluo vellere vexit ovem.
> o utinam, ne quis remo freta longa moveret,
>   Argo funestas pressa bibisset aquas!

> [The trouble began when the pine-tree from Pelion's summit taught evil journeys to wondering waves, the reckless ship making its way among clashing rocks, bore the Golden Fleece. O would that, so no one ever plied the wide sea with an oar, the Argo had had a calamitous leak!] (lines 1–6)

The *exemplum* chosen by the speaker to convey his unhappiness at his mistress' impending departure is as ambiguous as it is hyperbolic. On the surface, the *exemplum* reinforces the speaker's sense of abandonment in its evocation of Jason's tragic abandonment of Medea. The implied correlation between the speaker and Medea, however, suggests that the speaker does not, in fact, imagine himself in a powerless and passive position. It is Medea who engineers the glorious and successful culmination of Jason's heroic journey; in fact it is Medea who ultimately pulls the strings in many of Jason's endeavors. Likewise, it is the *amator* who actively and exuberantly arranges the images of his mistress on both the sea and the shore, in a sense facilitating an imaginary voyage. The uninteresting way the *amator* imagines Corinna at home, staying in bed, reading books, and practicing her lute (*tutius est fouisse torum, legisse libellos, / Threiciam digitis increpuisse lyram,* lines 31 and 32) does little to further his argument that she should stay home, which reinforces the impression it is really her imagined voyage away from him which fuels his creative and erotic imaginations. Indeed, the speaker evokes vivid images of "battling winds," the waters of Scylla and Charybdis, the "deep blue of the harsh sea." These images, although portending danger, also evoke the excitement and thrill of heroic adventure; the sea voyage comes to life, and the speaker himself is aroused by the danger. And although he admonishes Corinna to "let others" tell her of dangers on the sea (*haec alii referant vos*), he clearly relishes narrating in detail the various perils that await her. In fact, the possibility of his mistress embarking on a "dangerous" voyage titillates him; the thrill of amatory pursuit accelerates when the mistress is not merely on the other side of a locked door but is potentially out of the lover's reach forever.

    Not only does the *amator* relate in detail the dangers of the sea, he also imagines his mistress feeling remorse as she looks upon the shore and faces inevitable destruction.

> Sero respicitur tellus, ubi fune soluto
>   currit in immensum panda carina salum;
> navita sollicitus cum ventos horret iniquos

> et prope tam letum, quam prope cernit aquam.
> quod si concussas Triton exasperet undas,
>   quam tibi sit toto nullus in ore color!
> tum generosa voces fecundae sidera Ledae
>   et "felix," dicas "quem sua terra tenet!"

> [Too late the land is seen, when the rope is loosened
> and the curved keel hastens to the boundless sea;
> when the anxious sailor shudders at hostile winds
> and sees death near, as near as he sees the water.
> But if Triton should provoke agitated waves,
> all the color in your face would leave!
> Then you would call the high-born stars, sons of
> fruitful Leda, and say, "Happy is she whom her own land
> holds!"] (lines 23–30)

The vivid imagery in these lines reinforces the sense that the speaker enjoys displaying his own artistry, an opportunity afforded by his mistress's potential voyage. But there is more. The *amator* pictures his mistress here in a state of enervation, evidenced by the image of her as devoid of all color in her face. Not only does he imagine Corinna debilitated and helpless, he also associates her happiness with containment and confinement. Indeed, the double images of Corinna as pale and as confined by the earth imply a kind of death. Her happiness, as the *amator* imagines it (and perhaps it is he who is *felix* at the prospect), seems to depend on a complete surrender to forces outside herself. As we saw in the previous chapter, Ovid's *amator* is aroused equally by imagining his mistress as helpless *and* as vigorously unconstrained. Here, the *amator* switches from his portrayal of a feeble and frail Corinna to one who is animated and fearless, recounting to him her adventures on the sea.

> Illic adposito narrabis multa Lyaeo—
>   paene sit ut mediis obruta navis aquis;
> dumque ad me properas, neque iniquae tempora noctis
>   nec te praecipites extimuisse Notos.

> [There, when the wine is poured, you will tell me many things—how your ship was nearly sunk in the midst of the waves; and how while you hastened to me, you feared neither hours of unfriendly night nor headlong winds from the south.] (lines 49–52)

Despite the binary portrayals of his mistress in this poem, what seems to excite the *amator* most is his fantasy of the reunion he will have with her.

Once he has carried her onto the shore and they have exchanged passionate kisses and embraces, he joyfully imagines himself being entrapped by her verbal deceptions:

> omnia pro veris credam, sint ficta licebit:
>   cur ego non votis blandiar ipse meis?
> haec mihi quam primum caelo nitidissimus alto
>   Lucifer admisso tempora portet equo.

> [I'll believe everything you say, even if it is fiction: why shouldn't I myself be deluded by my own desires? May dazzlingly-bright Lucifer with his galloping celestial horse bring these moments to me as soon as possible.] (lines 53–56)

Leslie Cahoon reads the ending of the poem as evidence of the *amator*'s disillusionment once the fantasy of Corinna's return has reached its climax. She argues that the speaker is forced, at the end, to confront the "insurmountable obstacle of reality."[13] But I think that neither the tone of the speaker's fantasies nor the tone of the ending bears out such a reading. The *amator* does not confront reality at all. He brushes it aside completely and implies, by the way he exuberantly embraces Corinna's *ficta*, that he prefers deception to truth. Moreover, the final image of the most dazzling star (*Lucifer nitidissimus*) speeding across the sky not only evokes the excitement of the moment of Corinna's arrival but also suggests the creative spark that the *ficta* of her imagined voyage inspires in him.

Amores 2.19, 3.4, and 3.8

In 2.19, 3.4, and 3.8, Ovid shows further how deception is not only an inevitable part of the *amator*'s "love" but also how deception is, in fact, necessary to sustain it. In all three poems, which deal openly with adultery, the *amator*'s casual indifference to moral concerns becomes much more blatant. The lover's flaunting lack of consideration for the moral issues involved in adultery tears away the elegiac ideal that is predicated on the illusion of *fides*. Through the lover's attitudes, Ovid attempts to expose and ridicule the hypocrisy that is inherent in preserving that illusion. One of the ways he does this is by having the *amator* adopt contradictory attitudes toward the practice of husbands "pimping" for their wives. We see that the *amator*'s criteria for judging the husbands' behavior are based on the pursuit of his own pleasure and not on any moral or legal consideration.

In 2.19, the speaker clarifies for the husband of his mistress that deception is necessary for the speaker to feel love for her: *quo mihi fortunam, quae numquam fallere curet? / nil ego, quod nullo tempore laedat, amo.* [Why would anyone want a beautiful woman who never takes the trouble to deceive him? I couldn't love that which was never hurtful] (lines 6 and 7). Moreover, the speaker associates his capacity for love with being injured in some way (*laedat*). He emphasizes that what both generates and sustains love are mutual dominance and victimization. In addition, the speaker's use of the neuter form (*nil, quod*) for the object of his affections implies that love based on conquest also involves an objectification of the beloved. As he does in many of the elegies, the speaker cites examples from mythology to argue his point:

> pinguis amor nimiumque patens in taedia nobis
>   vertitur et, stomacho dulcis ut esca, nocet.
> si numquam Danaen habuisset aenea turris,
>   non esset Danae de Iove facta parens;
> dum servat Iuno mutatam cornibus Io,
>   facta est quam fuerat gratior illa Iovi.

[Love that is too comfortable and too accessible turns boring, and hurts the stomach like sweet food. If Danae hadn't been held in that bronze turret, would she have borne a child by Jove? When Juno set her watch over Io, who had been transformed into a horned heifer, she made her seem more desirable to Jove.] (lines 25–30)

Although the speaker seems to be advocating mutual deception and domination, the examples he chooses to make his point stress the victimization of the female lovers. In the cases of both Danae and Io, male sexual desire is linked explicitly to female captivity and silence. Even though the speaker encourages his mistress to deceive him and inflict physical pain on him, he can hardly be considered a victim. He is the one in control, attempting to orchestrate the way their affair will be conducted to satisfy his desires. Although the *amator* refers to his mistress as *versuta* (artful), it is he who ingeniously arranges what roles each of them will play to serve *his* desires best.

> saepe time simulans, saepe rogata nega;
>   et sine me ante tuos proiectum in limine postis
>   longa pruinosa frigora nocte pati.
> sic mihi durat amor longosque adolescit in annos;
>   hoc iuvat; haec animi sunt alimenta mei.

[Often feigning fear, often, when entreated, say no. And allow me to lie at your door and suffer long cold through the frosty night. Thus my love endures (grows hard), and ripens through long years; this gratifies, this is the food of my life.] (lines 20–26)

The *amator* implies not only that his sexual arousal depends on the use of deception but also that imagining himself in the role of suppliant at his mistress's door provokes pleasure rather than pain. The *amator* explicitly links his prostration and suffering with the heightening of his desires and sexual satisfaction. The emphasis on *his amor* and *his animus* implies that the reversible roles he imagines for himself and his mistress exist solely for *his* erotic and creative sustenance rather than hers. Further, the *amator* makes it clear that maintaining amatory relations depends on both deception and on a precarious balance of power: *si qua volet regnare diu, deludat amantem* [Deception is necessary for any woman, if she wants to rule over her lover for a long time] (line 33). Although the speaker is giving advice to his mistress about how she may dominate him through deception, the fact that he is fully aware of the deception and is the one manipulating her for his own pleasure makes her domination of him a sham. There is very little doubt about who dominates whom here.

The speaker is equally manipulative toward the husband of his mistress. He makes no pretense about his true motives for wanting the *maritus* to concern himself with the immorality of allowing his wife to have lovers:

at tu, formosae secure puellae,
    incipe iam prima claudere nocte forem;
incipe, quis totiens furtim tua limina pulset,
    quaerere, quid latrent nocte silente canes,
quas ferat et referat sollers ancilla tabellas,
    cur totiens vacuo secubat ipsa toro:
mordeat ista tuas aliquando cura medullas,
    daque locum nostris materiamque dolis.
ille potest vacuo furari litore harenas,
    uxorem stulti si quis amare potest.

[And as for you, careless of your lovely girl, why not start locking up at night, and start asking who knocks frequently at your door in secret. Why do the dogs bark in the silent night, and what about those letters the clever maid delivers back and forth, why does your wife sleep alone in an empty bed so often? May worry eat away at you now and then, and you give me the opportunity and a reason for my deceptions. Loving the wife of a foolish man is like stealing sand off the beach.] (lines 37–46)

[Q]uid mihi cum facili, quid cum lenone marito? corrumpit vitio gaudia nostra suo. [What good to me is an easy, pimping husband? His vice spoils my fun] (lines 57 and 58). The speaker openly admits that the only reason he wants the *maritus* to become more vigilant is so that the excitement of his amatory pursuit will be increased, and he will have an opportunity to exercise his skills at deception.

In 3.4, the counterpart to 2.19, the *amator* reverses his position toward the *maritus* completely and admonishes him to loosen his control over his wife so that she may pursue any desires she might have for other men. At first, it seems that the *amator* is encouraging the husband to be more permissive with his wife so that she will be more chaste. The *amator* argues that people naturally rebel against restrictions and desire whatever is forbidden:

> ut iam servaris bene corpus, adultera mens est
>   nec custodiri, ne velit, ulla potest;
> nec corpus servare potes, licet omnia claudas:
>   omnibus occlusis intus adulter erit.
> cui peccare licet, peccat minus: ipsa potestas
>   semina nequitiae languidiora facit.
> desine, crede mihi, vitia inritare vetando;
>   obsequio vinces aptius illa tuo.
> vidi ego nuper equum contra sua vincla tenacem
>   ore reluctanti fulminis ire modo;
> constitit, ut primum concessas sensit habenas
>   frenaque in effusa laxa iacere iuba.
> nitimur in vetitam semper cupimusque negata.

[Though you keep a close watch over her body, her mind is adulterous; guarding her won't stop her desire. You won't be able to guard her body, even if you bolt all the doors and lock everything up, there will still be an adulterer. But if you are permissive with her, she'll stray less. She'll become bored, and the freedom will make her desire for affairs subside. Stop, believe me, prohibiting vice only exacerbates; with more indulgence, you'll be more effective. Lately I saw a tight-reined stallion angrily bolt like lightning; as soon as he felt the reins slacken and the bridle loosen on his flowing mane, he stood still. We always insist on what is prohibited, and desire what is forbidden.] (lines 5–17)

The *amator*'s credibility here is extremely suspect in light of the fact that in 2.19 he uses the same argument about "forbidden fruit" to persuade the husband to increase his watch so that the amatory pursuit would be more challenging.

A number of Ovidian critics have pointed out how Ovid's narrator in the *Amores* is willing to say whatever he feels is necessary to seduce his mistress and that if one strategy does not work, he, very often abruptly, changes his tone and his tactics accordingly.[14] Critics, however, although marveling at the *amator*'s virtuosity, have often failed to question the exploitative and ruthless attitudes that are embedded in the *amator*'s clever posturing. In 2.19 the narrator admits unabashedly that imagining his mistress held captive by her husband evokes desire in him. And although the *amator* reverses his position in 3.4 by asking the *maritus* to be more permissive with his wife, the woman is still treated as a commodity of exchange between her lover and her husband — with no agency or autonomy of her own. Thus, the *Amores* reinforce Irigaray's argument that the foundations of Western patriarchal culture are based on the exchange of women between men and that women are used as commodities in the sexual and economic marketplace: "Men make commerce *of* them (women), but they do not enter into any exchanges *with* them."[15]

In his book *The Elementary Structures of Kinship*, Lévi-Strauss argues that in traditional cultures it is women who are the most precious objects of exchange among men.[16] These exchanges, Lévi-Strauss maintains, occur between men from one family group to another and thus help to establish relationships beyond the family, relationships that initiate social organization. In discussing these theories of the role of marriage in kinship systems, Gayle Rubin points out that the exchange of women by men in the marital union establishes a relationship between men which is based on reciprocity as well as on a kinship that consolidates a social link between the partners of the exchange, and thereby bestows power as well as social organization.

> If it is the women who are being transacted, then it is the men who give and take them who are linked, the woman being a conduit of a relationship rather than a partner to it.... If women are the gifts, then it is men who are the exchange partners. And it is the partners, not the presents, upon whom reciprocal exchange confers its quasi-mystical power of social linkage. The relations of such a system are such that women are in no position to realize the benefits of their own circulation.... "Exchange of women" is a shorthand for expressing that the social relations of a kinship system specify that men have certain rights in their female kin, and that women do not have the same rights either to themselves or to their male kin. In this sense, the exchange of women is a profound perception of a system in which women do not have full rights to themselves.[17]

In the *Amores*, however, Ovid does not portray the exchange of women between men in the context of accepted social norms but rather in the context of adulterous practices. In so doing, Ovid is able to highlight the way in which the use of women as a bartering commodity between men may be regarded not as a function of culture and sophistication but as an indication of moral degeneracy in the culture. By portraying such exchanges in the context of the kind of sexual "pandering" that goes on between the *amator* and the *maritus*, Ovid is able to reveal the crassness and commercialism that are inherent in using women as objects of exchange and how those exchanges contribute to the exploitation of women as well as the perpetuation of social values that emphasize perverse forms of commercialism in general. Ovid seems to suggest here that the *amator*'s attempts at pandering are part of a highly cultured system of trade and commerce.[18]

In both *Amores* 2.19 and 3.4, Ovid's *amator* tries to strike deals with the *maritus* of his mistress in order to manipulate how she will be used as an object of the *amator*'s pleasure. Indeed, an important aspect of the transactions between the *amator* and the *maritus* is the way those transactions point up how the subordination of women is a product of the relationships by which sex and gender are organized in Augustan culture. Ovid's poems demonstrate how the asymmetric division of the sexes is played out through their different roles as exchanger and exchanged and how those roles require control over women's sexuality. Ovid's metaphor for woman as a spirited horse needing to be controlled—whether through permissiveness or discipline—emphasizes the extent to which control over women's sexuality is a necessary element in establishing men's dominance over women. Women are portrayed not only as merchandise to be exchanged but also as tools in the process of establishing male relationships of mutual interest and solidarity. Although Ovid's *amator* appears to engage the *maritus* in order to have a relationship with a *puella*,[19] it is clear that it is the males who are both partners and beneficiaries in the process of exchange and that women are merely the vehicles of that exchange.[20] Moreover, the disparity between exchanger and exchanged, giver and gift, is reinforced in both poems in the way the sexual arousal of the *amator* is linked to male fantasies of control over a powerless and captive mistress.

In 3.4 the speaker uses the same mythological *exempla* he uses in 2.19 to try to persuade the husband, but for the opposite reason. In 2.19 the narrator uses Io and Danae as *exempla* of how women should be treated. He argues that women are more desirable if they are held in captivity and are rendered incapable of speaking for themselves. In 3.4 the speaker uses the examples of Io and Danae to show how women should not be treated, and he adds the example of Penelope to suggest that if the husband stops guarding his wife she will be as faithful as Penelope: *Penelope mansit, quamvis custode carebat, / inter tot iuvenes intemerata procos* [Penelope endured, although she lacked a guard, / chaste among so many youthful suitors] (lines 23 and 24). By including Penelope to support his argument, the speaker offers a paradigm for the wife which would be difficult to refuse. The narrator's willingness to use the same argument and *exempla* for contradictory purposes suggests that his concern for the chastity of free-born wives is a pose to suit his desires of the moment. Although the *amator*'s arguments in 2.19 and 3.4 are contradictory, the mythological examples of Io and Danae in both poems present women as most desirable when they have been dehumanized and exploited by male captors. The image of Penelope, although emphasizing female chastity, also calls attention to the fact that men have rights in determining the fate of women's sexuality which women themselves do not have.

The falseness of the *amator*'s concern for virtue becomes more blatant when he announces to the husband that it is simply unsophisticated to object to adulterous wives: *rusticus est nimium, quem laedit adultera coniunx* [That man is so provincial, who is hurt by an adulterous wife] (line 37). Here the *amator* explicitly associates being "cultured" with men's control over women's sexuality. Cultural sophistication is linked to the willingness to participate in what may be regarded as "primitive" rituals of exchange and reciprocity. Indeed, Gayle Rubin points out that the exchange of women in marriage is by no means confined to primitive societies. Rather, Rubin argues, "these practices seem only to become more pronounced and commercialized in more 'civilized' societies."[21] Ovid's amatory poems lend support to Rubin's view. In Augustan society the exchange of women between men is part of a social structure in which the woman is subject either to the powers of the *pater familias* or to another male guardian, whether it be a husband or other male relative.[22] If relations between men—exemplified by fathers and sons—ensures the genealogy of patriarchal power, then the exchange of women between men is central in the production of culture. Ovid takes this paradigm further and shows that the exchange of women goes beyond the "acceptable" social practices of passing women from fathers to sons. Here, Rubin's view that the exchange of women by men becomes more commercialized in sophisticated cultures is reinforced by the way Ovid shows how amatory rhetoric is itself a form of commerce, an instrument in the processes of exchange which help consolidate male hegemony. Moreover, the primacy of male relationships in Augustan culture, implicit in the *amator*'s transactions with the *maritus* of his mistress, suggest also that homosocial bonds between men can be seen as the basis of the socio-cultural order. By portraying women as goods in the "trade that organizes patriarchal society," Ovid reinforces the association of women with material culture. Women are the raw materials of the transactions men conduct with one another to manage sexual desire in the culture and ensure their own privileged status and supremacy over women.

The *amator* takes his argument even further, however, and asserts that Rome was, in fact, founded on adulterous practices:

> et notos mores non satis Urbis habet,
>   in qua Martigenae non sunt sine crimine nati
> Romulus Iliades Iliadesque Remus.
>
> [and he (the husband) doesn't recognize the character for which Rome is famous. Romulus and Remus, Ilia's Martian twins, weren't born without guilt.] (lines 38–40)

The implication in these lines is that if the *maritus* wants to be a good Roman, he had better adhere to the *vitia* that produced Rome in the first place. Indeed, one of the central myths in the story of the origins of Rome is the rape of the Sabine women. By having his *amator* encourage husbands to "pimp" for their wives and justify it by alluding to a "heroic" tradition that sanctions brutality toward women, Ovid presents a view of Roman society which includes a pervasive acceptance of deception and exploitation as an inevitable part of amatory relations, including marriage. By constructing an argument in favor of adultery from the perspective of how it will benefit the husband, Ovid reveals how easy it is to rationalize corrupt practices. Further, by having his *amator* link sexual pandering with Roman imperial conquests, Ovid suggests a close alliance between male sexual dominance and the assertion of political control and aggression.

In 3.8 the *amator* appears to reverse his moral indifference to the practice of pimping. Here, the *amator* expresses outrage that his mistress can be seduced by the allure of wealth and status and that, in essence, her affections can be bought:

> Et quisquam ingenuas etiam nunc suspicit artes
>   aut tenerum dotes carmen habere putat?
> ingenium quondam fuerat pretiosius auro,
>   at nunc barbaria est grandis habere nihil.
> cum pulchrae dominae nostri placuere libelli,
>   quo licuit libris, non licet ire mihi;
> cum bene laudavit, laudato ianua clausa est:

> turpiter huc illuc ingeniosus eo.
> ecce recens dives parto per vulnera censu
> praefertur nobis sanguine pastus eques.

[Does anyone nowadays admire liberal arts, or think that love poetry rates a dowry? At one time talent was more precious than gold, but now it is very uncivilized to have nothing. When my little books pleased my lovely mistress, it was possible for them to go where I couldn't. Once she has praised them, she shuts the door on the poet: Here and there I go, my talent disgraced. Look, a new-rich soldier whose wealth was acquired through violence and who was fed on slaughter is preferred to me.] (lines 1–10)

The *amator* presents himself as the upholder of ideals of purity in contrast to the crass values of commercialism. In 3.4 he associated being cultured with the cynical acceptance of a mercantilist approach to "love," but here the *amator* bemoans the degeneration of a culture that values money more than *ingenium*. The panderer we saw in 2.19 and 3.4 is now the *Musarumpurus Phoebique sacerdos* (line 23). When the *amator*'s high-minded moral position does not get him anywhere, however, he seeks ways in which to rationalize compromising his principles to succeed with his mistress:

> Iuppiter, admonitus nihil esse potentius auro,
> corruptae pretium, virginia ipse fuit.
> dum merces aberat, durus pater, ipsa severa,
> aerati postes, ferrea turris erat;
> sed postquam sapiens in munere venit adulter,
> praebuit ipsa sinus et dare iussa dedit.

[Jupiter, realizing that nothing is more powerful than gold, made himself the price offered to a corrupt virgin. While there was no profit, Father was tough, and the girl strict, her door-posts bronze, her tower iron. But after the clever seducer came in gifts, she offered herself and gave what she was commanded to give.] (lines 29–34)

As he does in a number of the elegies, the *amator* uses Jupiter as his model of a successful seducer of women. Violence, deception, and prostitution are all approaches employed by Jupiter which the *amator* emulates and uses as justifications for his own selfish ends. Here, the *exemplum* proves that women can be bought and that all the *sapiens adulter* needs is enough money. Jupiter's example is used to show that if one wants to be *sapiens*, one must be willing to abandon moral principles. In fact, the whole amatory enterprise is portrayed as corrupt. *Puellae* willingly give up their virtue for profit, and smart seducers will buy their way into the affections of their mistresses. The *amator*'s use of an *exemplum* to justify such corrupt practices reveals his moral outrage to be a sham—a device for seducing his *puella* away from a soldier made appealing because of his greater wealth and status. We find out that the *amator* is not upset about pandering for *moral* reasons but rather because he cannot afford the price:

> tantum ne nostros avidi liceantur amores
>   et (satis est) aliquid pauperis esse sinant.
> at nunc, exaequet tetricas licet illa Sabinas,
>   imperat ut captae, qui dare multa potest.
> me prohibet custos, in me timet illa maritum;
>   si dederim, tota cedet uterque domo.

> [So long as they don't bid up the prices on our lovers, and leave something for the pauper, it's enough. But now, even if my mistress were on a par with the Sabines, he who is able to give many gifts rules her as his captive. The watchman won't let me in, in my case she's afraid of her husband. If I could pay, they'd both leave us the house.] (lines 59–64)

Although the *amator* idealizes Jupiter's amatory practices, he also announces that his standard for judging a woman's "worth" is how she measures up to one of the Sabine women. His ideal woman—too costly for him at the moment—is one who offers the greatest opportunity for him to subjugate her. Earlier in the *Amores*, in 1.3, the *amator* expressed similar sentiments (only veiled in mythological allusion) when he used Jupiter's relationships with Io, Leda, and Europa as examples of ideal amatory unions. The *amator*'s implied correlation of an ideal mistress with mythical women in 1.3 becomes blatant admission in many of the elegies in the third book. In 3.8, the *amator* makes it clear at the end that everyone is out for profit. For the right price, the husband, with the *custos* as accomplice, would turn his home into a house of prostitution.

Amores 3.12

In 3.12 the theme of the exploitation of women for profit is heightened when the *amator* admits that he has prostituted his mistress for the sake of his literary fame. He begins by complaining that his own verses are causing him trouble because they have publicized the charms of his *puella* and made other men desire her:

> Quis fuit ille dies, quo tristia semper amanti
> omina non albae concinuistis aves?
> quodue putem sidus nostris occurrere fatis,
> quosve deos in me bella movere querar?
> quae modo dicta mea est, quam coepi solus amare,
> cum multis vereor ne sit habenda mihi.

[What day was it when you evil birds sang the eternally sad omens of love? What star of fate has crossed over me? What gods cause trouble for me I lament? She who was recently mine, she whom I started to love alone, I fear I must share her with the multitude.] (lines 1–6)

The *amator*'s stance as the helpless victim of an obsession with *one* woman is contradicted by his declaration in other elegies that he desires a multitude of beautiful women. In addition, the sudden change from the idealized perspective of the elegiac lover to an emphasis on the mercantile aspects of love undermines the *amator*'s credibility.

The *amator*'s position of complaint that Corinna is "on the market" now because of him is undermined by the underlying implication that he has profited from her as his *subject* in his elegies. What is really on the market are the elegies themselves. Like a pimp, he has profited from his "sale" of her to other lovers, not in monetary terms, but in terms of literary fame. The extent to which he is carried away by imagining other men gaining access to his mistress reveals excitement, rather than outrage, at having the ability to make Corinna seem so desirable. The *amator* admits openly that by making his mistress an attractive and therefore highly marketable commodity, he has become a panderer himself:

> fallimur, an nostris innotuit illa libellis?
> sic erit: ingenio prostitit illa meo.
> et merito: quid enim formae praeconia feci?
> vendibilis culpa facta puella mea est.
> me lenone placet, duce me perductus amator,
> ianua per nostras est adaperta manus.
> an prosint dubium, nocuerunt carmina certe:
> invidiae nostris illa fuere bonis.

[Am I deceived, or could it be that she has become well-known because of my books? That's it: she was prostituted by my genius. It serves me right: why was I the one who proclaimed her beauty? It is my fault that my girl has gone up for sale. I have been the panderer of her charms, I have led other lovers to her, and it was I who opened the doors for them. The benefit my poems have brought me is dubious; they've certainly caused me trouble, and made people envy my success.] (lines 7–14)

The *amator*'s entire argument is based on a view of the *puella* as a commodity for him to possess or sell to others. Here he imagines an alliance not with a *maritus* but with an audience of men in general. Whereas earlier the woman is presented as the object of a transaction between her lover and her husband, now she is inseparable from the poems offered as gifts to a voyeuristic and lascivious audience of men. The *puella*'s identity as a woman, even a subordinated one, has been subsumed entirely by her role as a literary construction in the *amator*'s poems.

In 1.3, in the context of manipulating his mistress with promises of *fama*, the *amator* asked her to give herself to him as *materia* for his *carmina: te mihi materiem felicem in carmina praebe* (line 19). But in 1.3 the *amator*'s identification of the woman as *materia* is veiled by his conventional elegiac rhetoric of subservience toward her.[23] In 3.12 the *amator* is entirely forthright in his presentation of the elegiac mistress as a thing of sale. The elegiac poet is a panderer who uses her as a *vehicle* to display his talents and sell poems, and her marketability is linked closely to the arousal of male sexual desire, both in the *amator* himself and in the fantasies he has of other men sharing her with him. The *amator*'s presentation of his mistress as *vendibilis* defines her exclusively in terms of her *function*—a vehicle of exchange between a male poet and an audience of sexually excitable, predatory men. The pimping we saw in the *amator* trying to make deals with the *maritus* of his mistress now becomes pandering on a large scale. The sexuality of the *femina* is entirely "owned" by the men who use her as an object of exchange.

Moreover, the *amator*'s complaints about having to share Corinna with other men contradict his insistence in other poems that the presence of rivals or, for that matter, obstacles in general, only increases the thrill of the amatory pursuit and fuels his creative imagination as well. Immediately after denouncing his own talents in 3.12, the *amator* spends half of the poem offering a display of his poetic virtuosity. He enumerates in stunning detail some of the most well-known myths (e.g., Scylla, Tantalus, Niobe, Proteus) that he, along with other poets, has brought to life in verse. If the *amator*'s ulterior motive in this poem is to win back the affections of his mistress, then he is very clever. His pose of pretending to be sorry that he made Corinna so famous conceals his more subtle strategy of dazzling both her and his audience with his genius. Like Jupiter showering gold, the *amator* showers his readers with his gilded rhetoric of myth making:

Sexual Politics in Ovid's *Amores*

21 per nos Scylla patri caros furata capillos
      pube premit rabidos inguinibusque canes;
  nos pedibus pinnas dedimus, nos crinibus angues;
      victor Abantiades alite fertur equo.
  idem per spatium Tityon porreximus ingens
26   et tria vipereo fecimus ora cani;
  fecimus Enceladon iaculantem mille lacertis,
      ambiguae captos virginis ore viros;
  Aeolios Ithacis inclusimus utribus Euros;
      proditor in medio Tantalus amne sitit;
31 de Niobe silicem, de virgine fecimus ursam;
      concinit Odrysium Cecropis ales Ityn;
  Iuppiter aut in aves aut se transformat in aurum
      aut secat imposita virgine taurus aquas.
  Protea quid referam Thebanaque semina dentes;
36   qui vomerent flammas ore, fuisse boves,
  flere genis electra tuas, auriga, sorores,
      quaeque rates fuerint, nunc maris esse deas,
  aversumque diem mensis furialibus Atrei,
      duraque percussam saxa secuta lyram?
41 exit in immensum fecunda licentia vatum
      obligat historica nec sua verba fide.

[It was because of us poets that Scylla ravaged her father's locks, and keeps packs of mad dogs in her groin and womb. We gave wings to feet, put snakes in hair, made Pegasus strong, carried by his wings. We stretched Tityos out over an enormous space, made three heads for the venomous dog; made Enceladus, shooting spears with his thousand arms, made heroes ravished by the voice of the two-formed Sirens. We shut up the winds of Aeolus in a wineskin for Odysseus, because of us treacherous Tantalus thirsts in the middle of the river, we turned Niobe to flint, made a she-bear from a virgin, Procne into a nightingale. We let Jupiter transform himself into a bird or into gold or as a bull cut the sea with a virgin on his back. Why should I call to mind Proteus, the Theban sown teeth of the dragon, the oxen snorting flames from their mouths, Phaethon's sisters weeping amber tears, sea-goddesses conjured from ships, and the sun turned away from the sight of Thyestes' frenzied feast, and harsh rocks inspired by the sound of the lyre. Poetic license is boundless, and isn't constrained by historical accuracy.]

    All of the *amator*'s mythological *exempla* bear witness to the poet's abilities to make illusion seem like reality. The *amator*'s long list of myths is a devious way of praising the poet's talents. The *amator* demonstrates how easy it is to be seduced by the poet's myth making, by his powers of language which make mythological figures seem real. But underlying the *amator*'s inventory of the poet's accomplishments is an elaborate deception of both his mistress and his audience. He wears the mask of the abandoned lover and pretends to prefer reality to fiction, but we have seen the way he celebrates at great length the fictional world of myth created by the poet. Like his myths, Corinna is also a fiction created by the poet, and the implication is that if she continues to be a fiction—that is, *materia* for the poet to use for his art—she will gain mythical status. The *amator*'s strategy is ingenious, both as a means of winning back his mistress and as a way of showing off his skills as a poet. The *amator*'s assertion that the "gullibility" (*credulitas*) of his audience has been harmful to him is hardly believable, considering his own argument that his genius has produced such compelling and seductive images of his *femina*.

At line 41, the *amator* refers to the poet's skills as *fecunda licentia*, a description that, on one level, may be interpreted as *poetic license*. Poetic license by itself is a gender-neutral activity that normally refers to the poet's authority to manipulate language freely and creatively. But here the basic meaning of *fecunda* as *fertile* resonates with the *amator*'s earlier allusions to his mistress as fertile *materia* for his poetic productions. Furthermore, the sexual overtones of *licentia* suggest a link between the poetic license of the elegiac poet and the wanton use of the *materia* for his art. In other words, the poet exploits the fertile subject of woman to produce his *carmina* as his offspring. Far from being his undoing, the success of the *amator*'s pandering has proven what a fruitful enterprise literary prostitution can be. Showing how good a salesman the *amator* is, Ovid suggests that the elegiac stance of servitude toward the mistress is self-serving for the *amator* and dehumanizing toward women. Moreover, by having his *amator* openly identify the elegiac mistress as *materia*, Ovid points to an objectification and exploitation of the female which are inherent not only in the elegiac enterprise but in the nature of amatory relations in general.

Roman poets before Ovid showed the connection between sexual and political conquest, and they criticized the values of commercialism which were so prominent in Roman society. Both Catullus and Propertius dramatize the conflict between the private world of the lover and the *vita activa* of the statesman and the soldier. But for both poets, the erotic and imaginative life offers, at least potentially, a moral refuge from the degradation in the exterior world. Ovid, on the other hand, shows that rather than provide a moral alternative, *amor* often reiterates the mercantilist and imperialist values in Roman society. His elegies expose the competitive and violent nature of love and show how erotic warfare is as potentially threatening to the social order, to the perpetuation of cultural ideals, as actual warfare. By exhibiting how dehumanizing the male lover's conquest of his beloved is, Ovid permits us to see the destructiveness and inhumanity in the desire to conquer and enslave others.

Further, Ovid's portrayal of the poet in the *Amores* seems, on the surface, to disavow the idealism traditionally associated with poets of love. But Ovid's demystification of the elegiac poet's avowed commitment to moral ideals questions and destabilizes ideologies of erotic conquest and domination. In refusing to perpetuate the illusions and self-deceptions that he believed were so much a part of love and love poetry, Ovid's poems reflect a deep commitment to the moral responsibility of the poet to show the cruelty and inhumanity perpetrated in the name of culture, in the name of *amor*.

Notes

Introduction

1. A complete list of works published on women in antiquity and on gender in the ancient world would be enormous. Included is a selection that can lead the reader to other publications in the field: Léonie Archer, Susan Fischler, and Maria Wyke, eds., *Women in Ancient Societies;* Averil Cameron and Amelie Kuhrt, eds., *Images of Women in Antiquity;* Eva Cantarella, *Pandora's Daughters;* Page duBois, *Sowing the Body;* Elaine Fantham et al., eds., *Women in the Classical World;* Helene Foley, ed., *Reflections of Women in Antiquity;* Jane F. Gardner, *Women in Roman Law and Society;* Mary R. Lefkowitz and Maureen Fant, eds., *Women's Life in Greece and Rome;* John Peradotto and J. P. Sullivan, eds., *Women in the Ancient World;* Sarah B. Pomeroy, *Goddesses, Whores, Wives, and Slaves;* Idem, *Women's History and Ancient History;* Nancy Sorkin Rabinowitz and Amy Richlin, eds., *Feminist Theory and the Classics;* Adele Scafuro and Eva Stehle, eds., "Studies on Roman Women"; Marilyn Skinner, "Rescuing Creusa"; John J. Winkler, *The Constraints of Desire.*

2. Jane Flax, "Postmodernism and Gender Relations," 629.

3. Ibid., 627.

4. As Jane Flax maintains, "gender relations so far as we have been able to understand them have been (more or less) relations of domination. That is, gender relations have been (more) defined and (imperfectly) controlled by one of their interrelated aspects—the man" ("Postmodernism and Gender Relations," 629).

5. See, especially, Leslie Cahoon, "Let the Muse Sing On"; Barbara Gold, "'But Ariadne Was Never There in the First Place'"; Judith Hallett, "The Role of Women in Roman Elegy"; Amy Richlin, "Reading Ovid's Rapes"; Maria Wyke, "Written Women"; Idem, "Mistress and Metaphor in Augustan Elegy."

6. See Ronnie Ancona, "The Subterfuge of Reason," 50–51. In her examination of desire in *Odes* 1.23, Ancona offers a very convincing critique of a scholarly approach that ignores the gender specificity of desire in Horace's poem, a critique that may be applied usefully to scholarship on Latin love poetry in general.

CHAPTER ONE. The Catullan Ego: Fragmentation and the Erotic Self

Ideas presented in this chapter were first expressed in an article "The Catullan Ego: Fragmentation and the Erotic Self." *American Journal of Philology* 116 (1995): 77–94.

1. See, especially, J. A. Barsby, "Rhythmical Factors in Catullus"; Steele Commager, "Notes on Some Poems of Catullus"; Frank Copley, "Emotional Conflict and Its Significance in the Lesbia Poems of Catullus"; J. P. Elder, "Notes on Some Conscious and Unconscious Elements in Catullus' Poetry"; Eduard Fraenkel, "Two Poems of Catullus"; R. O. A. M. Lyne, *The Latin Love Poets;* Michael Putnam, ed., *Essays on Latin Lyric, Elegy, and Epic*, 13–29; Kenneth Quinn, *Approaches to Catullus;* Carl Rubino, "The Erotic World of Catullus."

2. For a helpful discussion of the divisions between logic and emotion in Catullus' poetry, see Paul Allen Miller, "Catullus, C. 70."

3. See also David Konstan, "Two Kinds of Love in Catullus."

4. See Daniel Selden, "*Ceveat lector.*" Selden's essay is important in bringing to light the diverse, contradictory readings that Catullus' poetry has generated. As Selden insightfully observes, "The formalized and repetitive patterning of Catullus' grammar obtrudes not only as an operation independent of whatever content it conveys; however one construes the sentence, its syntax leaves a remainder which, far from being exhausted in the meaning, undoes the possibility of determining the sense. . . . In Catullus' poetry, however, parsing produces the effect of an unresolved semantic fluctuation, and this inevitably vitiates the project of delineating anything about its subject that is certain." Selden's emphasis on the ambiguity of both the meaning in Catullus' texts and the persona in the poems makes a useful contribution to Catullan scholarship. My argument, however, shows that it is precisely the ambiguity and irresolution that *are* the meaning in Catullus' poems. Indeed, what Selden calls the "undecidability" in the Catullan corpus is the heart of Catullus' enactment of the inherent ambivalence of the lover's position and of amatory experience in general. In other words, Catullus dramatizes for us the painful coexistence of irreconcilable positions in the lover and in erotic discourse.

5. For a useful discussion of the concepts of person/persona, individual/self in light of Catullus' divided consciousness, see Micaela Janan, "*When the Lamp Is Shattered*," x, 5–6.

6. For a linguistic discussion of pronominal patterning in lyric discourse, see Emile Benveniste, *Problems in General Linguistics*. For an analysis of "lyric pronouns" and their origin in ancient lyric, see W. R. Johnson, *The Idea of Lyric*, 1–23.

7. For other examples of Catullus' use of multiple speaking voices, see, in particular, Poems 11, 51, 79, 83, and 85.

8. See R. L. Rowland, "*Miser Catulle.*" Rowland acknowledges that Poem 8 is a dialogue between two distinct voices, the irrational lover and the rational speaker. But he insists that the dialogue indicates that the poet himself is a detached observer of the struggle between speaker and lover. See also Marilyn Skinner, "Catullus 8," 300. Skinner says that she understands "Catullus the poet to employ his material as a 'distancing device,' so that the speaker of the poem becomes both a projection of and a means of control over his own turbulent feelings." For a discussion of the dichotomy

between lover and poet in Poem 8, see Peter Connor, "Catullus 8." Connor takes the view that "Catullus does not harshly set up two poles which rigidly focus diametrically opposed personalities.... We see rather, in lively existence, two aspects of an indivisible personality." Connor neither examines the pronominal patterning in the poem, nor does he consider that Catullus presents the erotic self as essentially fragmented. For a discussion of diverse voices in Poem 8, see John Newman, *Roman Catullus and the Modification of the Alexandrian Sensibility*, 158–60.

9. Eduard Fraenkel, "*Vesper Adest,*" 6.
10. Roland Barthes, *A Lover's Discourse*, 15.
11. See Eve Adler, *Catullan Self-Revelation*, 8–12.
12. For discussions of sexual role reversals in Catullus' poetry, see William Fitzgerald, *Catullan Provocations*, especially Chapter 7; Ernst Fredricksmeyer, "The Beginning and the End of Catullus' *Longus Amor*"; Judith Hallett, "The Role of Women in Roman Elegy"; Paul Allen Miller, *Lyric Texts and Lyric Consciousness*, especially Chapter 6; David Mulroy, "An Interpretation of Catullus 11"; Michael Putnam, "Catullus 11"; Kenneth Quinn, *Approaches to Catullus;* Carl Rubino, "The Erotic World"; Eva Stehle, "Retreat from the Male"; David Sweet, "Catullus 11."
13. Roland Barthes, *A Lover's Discourse*, 13–14.
14. See Catharine Edwards' analysis of Roman moralizing discourse, *The Politics of Immorality in Ancient Rome*.
15. Ibid., 26.
16. See J. N. Adams, *The Latin Sexual Vocabulary*.
17. For a discussion of Catullus' comparison of his love for Lesbia with paternal love, see Daniel Harmon, "Catullus 72.3–4," 321–22.
18. For a fuller discussion of this argument, see Carl Rubino, "The Erotic World of Catullus."
19. For an analysis of Catullus' use of political speech in his erotic poems, see Marilyn Skinner, "Parasites and Strange Bedfellows."
20. Marilyn Skinner, "Disease Imagery in Catullus 76.17–26." Skinner offers a fruitful discussion of how Catullus employs images of disease to describe his emotional condition.
21. W. R. Johnson, *The Idea of Lyric*, 122.

CHAPTER TWO. Gendered Domains: Public and Private in Catullus

1. See Micaela Janan's discussion of the two poles in the construction of Woman— as either "demonized whore" or "exalted goddess" in Chapters 1–3. Janan writes, "Man erects a number of conjectures around Woman. One such guess is misogyny—resentment at the impossibility of the sexual relation relegated to Woman's side of the equation, as fantasized whore, castrating bitch, and the like. Another is courtly love—the rendering of the impossibility as Woman's inaccessibility, her elevation into the position of distant, goddesslike being" (71).
2. Ibid., Chapter 2, especially 58–62.
3. See Marilyn Skinner's discussion of constructions of male sexuality in Catullus in "*Ego Mulier.*" Skinner argues that Catullus' reappropriation of the "outlawed

feminine" presented an alternative subject position "permitting scope for voluptuous emotive fancy." Moreover, Skinner maintains that male identification with "feminine" helplessness was a basic component in the construction of Roman male sexuality.

4. Elaine Showalter's essay, "Introduction: The Rise of Gender," is a useful introduction to the ways in which gender studies have developed out of feminist criticism.

5. The texts of both Catullus 5 and 11 are taken from Kenneth Quinn, *Catullus: The Poems*. The English translations of the poems are my own.

6. Charles Segal, "Catullus 5 and 7," 288. Segal provides an illuminating discussion of the important relationship between sound and meaning in Poems 5 and 7.

7. Micaela Janan argues, "As if she has gone over to the enemy camp—those grim ancients with the minds of bookkeepers—Lesbia herself wants him to submit a request for an *exact* number of kisses" ("*When the Lamp Is Shattered*," 60).

8. For a discussion of the traditional association between femininity and materiality in Western thought, see Judith Butler, *Bodies That Matter*, especially Chapter 1.

9. Aristotle, "*De Anima*."

10. Page duBois, *Sowing the Body*, especially Chapters 6 and 7.

11. See Val Plumwood, "Women, Humanity, and Nature," 212.

12. Teresa de Lauretis, *Technologies of Gender*, 43.

13. Micaela Janan, "*When the Lamp Is Shattered*," 62.

14. See E. D. Blodgett and Rosemary Nielsen, "Mask and Figure in Catullus, *Carmen* 11"; D. F. Bright, "*Non Bona Dicta*"; P. Y. Forsyth, "Thematic Unity of Catullus 11"; Ernst Fredricksmeyer, "The Beginning and the End of Catullus' *Longus Amor*"; Idem, "Method and Interpretation"; T. E. Kinsey, "Catullus 11"; David McKie, "The Horrible and Ultimate Britons"; David Mulroy, "An Interpretation of Catullus 11"; Michael Putnam, "Catullus 11"; Kenneth Quinn, *Catullus: The Poems*; L. Richardson, "*Furi et Aureli, Comites Catulli*"; R. T. Scott, "On Catullus 11"; David Sweet, "Catullus 11"; J. C. Yardley, "Catullus 11.7–8."

15. Ernst Fredricksmeyer, "Method and Interpretation," 94.

16. Ibid., 98.

17. Ibid., 95.

18. See Eve Adler, *Catullan Self-Revelation*, 18 ff.

19. Ernst Fredricksmeyer, "The Beginning and the End of Catullus' *Longus Amor*," 75.

20. E. D. Blodgett and Rosemary Nielsen, "Mask and Figure in Catullus, *Carmen* 11," 25.

21. The images the speaker uses to describe his future journey are, as David Sweet says, "images which call attention to themselves and in doing so distract from one's psychic distress" ("Catullus 11," 519).

22. For an interpretation of the images in the catalogue as erotic, see Michael Putnam, "Catullus 11," 15; T. E. Kinsey, "Catullus 11," 540–41; David Sweet, "Catullus 11," 520; and J. C. Yardley, "Catullus 11.7–8," 143.

23. See David Sweet, "Catullus 11," 520. Sweet argues that although the speaker's catalogue does not contain explicit sexuality, "in any case, we might respond to these images as of the stock metaphor of the river or flood-tide of passion."

24. Micaela Janan, "*When the Lamp Is Shattered*," 64.

25. See Kenneth Quinn's notes on Poem 11 in *Catullus: The Poems*, 125–30; see also

Charles Martin's notes on the references to place in the poem in his translations of Catullus' poems, *The Poems of Catullus*, 161–62.

26. R. T. Scott points to the mythological figure of Scylla as Catullus' "ultimate source" for his description of Lesbia, "Thus it seems to me, Catullus drew on the fluid tradition concerning Scylla to shape the imagery and invective of his message to Lesbia. His picture deftly combines throughout the primordial, epic beast and the later, sexually wanton woman. . . . And the accomplishment involves no appreciable sacrifice of the elevated tone of the previous stanzas" ("On Catullus 11," 41).

27. In addition to the commentators already cited, see Eva Stehle (Stigers), "Retreat from the Male."

28. Micaela Janan, "*When the Lamp Is Shattered*," 65.

29. Ernst Fredricksmeyer, "The Beginning and the End of Catullus' *Longus Amor*," 73.

30. Michael Putnam, *Essays on Latin Lyric, Elegy, and Epic*, 22–23: "the simile is remarkable, helping us escape past the monster into a paradigm of nature destroyed."

31. Ibid., 21.

32. From the *Aeneid*, Book IX, lines 430–37:

talia dicta dabat, sed viribus ensis adactus
transabiit costas et candida pectora rumpit.
vovitur Euryalus leto, pulchrosque per artus
it cruor inque umeros cervix conlapsa recumbit:
purpureus veluti cum flos succisus aratro
lanquescit moriens, lassove papavera collo
demisere caput pluvia cum forte gravantur.

[So was he pleading when the sword, thrust home with force, pierced through the ribs and broke the white breast of Euryalus. He tumbles into death, the blood flows down his handsome limbs; his neck, collapsing, leans against his shoulder: even as a purple flower, severed by the plow, falls slack in death; or poppies as, with weary necks, they bow their heads when weighted down by sudden rain.] (Mandelbaum translation, lines 574–81)

33. Page duBois writes, "The observers, the witnesses, the beholders of the world have been both male and female, but only the male spectators, the *theoroi*, have been official ambassadors, named to see. They have seen, spoken, and written their desire" (*Sowing the Body*, 10).

CHAPTER THREE. Elegiac Woman: Fantasy, *Materia*, and Male Desire in Propertius' *Monobiblios*

A portion of this essay is contained in "Elegiac Woman: Fantasy, *Materia*, and Male Desire in Propertius 1.3 and 1.11." *American Journal of Philology* 116 (1995): 303–18.

1. For a lucid analysis of the elegiac figure of the *servitium amoris*, see R. O. A. M. Lyne, "*Servitium Amoris*." See also Frank Copley, "*Servitium Amoris*."

2. Maria Wyke, "Written Women"; Idem, "Mistress and Metaphor."

3. Georg Luck, *The Latin Love Elegy*.

4. See, for example, Sappho 31 and Catullus 51.

5. For an analysis of the ways in which *eros*, in Greek literature, is closely associated with "a loss of vital self," see Anne Carson, *Eros the Bittersweet*.

6. In the *Symposium*, Phaedrus uses the metaphor of the lover as soldier to describe the dedication and passion lovers have in relation to their objects of desire. To support his argument, Phaedrus uses the example of Achilles who makes "the heroic choice to go to the rescue of his lover Patroclus and to avenge him" (*Symposium*, 179c).

7. For examples in epic which show a victor putting his foot on the victim before despoiling him, see the *Iliad*, V.620; the *Iliad*, XIII.618 ff.; and the *Aeneid*, X.490 ff.

8. Hans-Peter Stahl, *Propertius: Love and War*.

9. A paradigm for this association is the figure of Paris in the *Iliad*. His ineffectual behavior on the battlefield, his sudden shift from the battlefield to the bed, and Hector's taunting of Paris all serve to reinforce this paradigm.

10. In "*Sunt Qui Propertium Malint*," 272–73, A. W. Allen comments on Propertius' attitude toward magic:

> But the connection of love and magic was firmly established in literature, and all the Roman elegists frequently introduce magic. There has been debate as to whether this is proof that the elegiac poets were genuinely convinced of the efficacy of magic, or were simply following a literary convention. If by genuine conviction is meant a normal and considered belief, it is not likely that Propertius, Tibullus, and Ovid accepted magic as having real validity. Belief in magic was, it is true, widespread in Rome, but the attitude of educated men has to be distinguished from that of the populace. . . . It is unlikely that members of so cultivated a society as that to which the Roman elegists belonged actually shared popular superstitions of this kind.

11. For some discussions of erotic magic, see Christopher Faraone, "The Wheel, the Whip, and Other Implements of Torture"; Idem, "Sex and Power"; C. A. Faraone and D. Obbink, eds., *Magika Hiera;* and Georg Luck, *Arcana Mundi*.

12. In line 24, L. Richardson uses *Cytaeines*, whereas Camps prefers *Cytinaeis*. The former, translated as "the woman of Cytae," would specifically evoke Medea. The latter, translated as Thessalian agreeing with *carminibus*, would in any case be associated with the place typically linked to Greek witches.

13. Christopher Faraone, "Sex and Power," 92.

14. Hans-Peter Stahl, *Propertius: Love and War*, 44.

15. Ibid.

16. In her essay "Is the Gaze Male?," E. Ann Kaplan, using terms borrowed from Lacan, notes that "woman cannot enter the world of the symbolic, of language. . . . In patriarchal structures, thus, woman is located as other (enigma, mystery), and is thereby viewed as outside of (male) language" (310).

17. See Karen Bassi's study of the elegiac persona in Tibullus 1.1, "Desired Silence."

18. In *The Bonds of Love*, Jessica Benjamin offers a highly illuminating, feminist analysis of the psychological underpinnings of erotic domination. Her discussion of the relation between gender and domination demonstrates the complex intertwining of sexual and social domination.

19. Luce Irigaray, "This Sex Which Is Not One." Irigaray's work has been ex-

tremely influential in articulating important ideas about the question of woman's *essence* and of a female sexuality.

20. Maria Wyke, "Mistress and Metaphor," 42–43.

21. Ibid., 42.

22. See, especially, A. W. Allen, "*Sunt Qui Propertium Malint*"; R. J. Baker, "Beauty and the Beast"; Leo Curran, "Vision and Reality"; F. M. Dunn, "The Lover Reflected in the *Exemplum*"; Daniel Harmon, "Myth and Fantasy"; R. O. A. M. Lyne, "Propertius and Cynthia."

23. R. O. A. M. Lyne, "Propertius and Cynthia," 61.

24. Daniel Harmon, "Myth and Fantasy," 152.

25. Leo Curran, "Vision and Reality," 200.

26. Ibid., 191. Curran observes, "In 1.1 and 1.2 Cynthia is introduced immediately, a context is established, and only then is she compared, or contrasted with, the heroines of mythology. In these two poems the world of elegy, with its circumscribed borders, is subsequently expanded in order to encompass the great world of the epic and the heroic. In 1.3, on the other hand, there is a reversal of this technique: the larger world is evoked at the beginning and then reduced to the narrower focus of elegy."

27. A. W. Allen, "*Sunt Qui Propertium Malint*," 134.

28. R. J. Baker, "Beauty and the Beast," 250. Baker's article provides a persuasive and lucid argument for seeing strong erotic implications in the language of the first three couplets.

29. See Ronnie Ancona, "The Subterfuge of Reason."

30. Daniel Harmon, "Myth and Fantasy," 153.

31. Leo Curran, "Vision and Reality," 196.

32. Daniel Harmon, "Myth and Fantasy," 155.

33. Leo Curran, "Vision and Reality," 194–95.

34. Ibid., 204.

35. Leo Curran holds the view that the speaker's gaze upon his mistress and his gestures toward her while she sleeps are indications of affectionate tenderness. This view, I believe, exhibits a blindness to the *male-specific* quality of the speaker's expressions of desire: "The implications, whether Io be conceived of as a heifer or simply as a girl with horns, poke gentle fun at both Cynthia and Propertius.... As Propertius turns from narration to the reader to apostrophize Cynthia herself.... All is intimacy and tenderness," 201–2.

36. See Daniel Harmon's remarks about the apple imagery in "Myth and Fantasy," 160.

37. Leo Curran, "Vision and Reality," 206.

38. See Val Plumwood's provocative essay, "Women, Humanity, and Nature." Plumwood argues that "the Western philosophical tradition which has identified, on the one hand, maleness with rationality, and on the other hand, femaleness with the sphere of nature, has provided one of the main intellectual bases for the domination of women in Western culture."

39. See Maria Wyke, "Mistress and Metaphor," 38–41; see also Marylin Arthur, "Early Greece."

40. Maria Wyke writes, "Consequently, in the conceptual framework of Roman society, female sexuality takes on positive value only when ordered in terms that will

be socially effective for patriarchy. Sexually unrestrained women are marginalized. Displaced from a central position in cultural categories, they are associated with social disruption ("Mistress and Metaphor," 39).

41. John Warden, *Fallax Opus*. See, especially, his last chapter on Propertius' use of apostrophe.

42. Maria Wyke, "Mistress and Metaphor," 41.

43. Ibid., 39.

44. See, especially, Sandra Lee Bartky, *Femininity and Domination;* Judith Butler, *Gender Trouble;* Diana Fuss, *Essentially Speaking,* 55–72; Toril Moi, *Sexual/Textual Politics,* 127–49; Elizabeth V. Spelman, *Inessential Woman,* especially ch. 3.

45. Barbara Gold posits the image of Cynthia as one that reflects a traditional role for women; "Cynthia's chief purpose is to play the "other" to Propertius's hero ... her position is relational and is defined entirely by the parts he plays" (" 'But Ariadne Was Never There in the First Place,' " 89).

46. See Jessica Benjamin's chapters, "The Oedipal Riddle," 133–82, and "Gender and Domination," in *The Bonds of Love,* 183–218.

47. Ibid., 214–15.

48. Ibid., 205.

CHAPTER FOUR. Ovid's *Amores:* Women, Violence, and Voyeurism

The epigraph is from Michel Foucault's *The History of Sexuality.* For his analysis of sexuality and power relations, see this influential three-volume work.

1. Two important volumes of *Helios* are devoted to a critical reevaluation of Ovid's works. *Helios* 12 (1985) contains Leslie Cahoon, "A Program for Betrayal," 29–39; Alison Goddard Elliot, "Ovid and the Critics," 9–19; Mary-Kay Gamel, "Introduction," 3–7; Julie Hemker, "Rape and the Founding of Rome," 41–47; W. R. Johnson, "Ringing Down the Curtain on Love," 21–29; Charles Segal, "Ovid: Metamorphosis, Hero, Poet," 49–64. *Helios* 17 (1990) devoted an entire issue to a discussion of "reading" women's lives in Ovid's poetry. The essays in these issues interrogate Ovid's works from a feminist perspective and offer many illuminating insights about reading Ovid in terms of gender. Especially important are Leslie Cahoon, "Let the Muse Sing On," 197–211; Phyllis Culham, "Decentering the Text," 161–70; Eva Keuls, "The Feminist View of the Past," 221–24; and Amy Richlin, "Hijacking the Palladion," 175–85.

2. See, especially, I. M. Le M. Du Quesnay, "The *Amores*"; Hermann Frankel, *Ovid, A Poet Between Two Worlds;* A. G. Lee, "*Tenerorum Lusor Amorum*"; Georg Luck, *The Latin Love Elegy;* Kenneth Quinn, *Latin Explorations;* and L. P. Wilkinson, *Ovid Recalled.*

3. As Leslie Cahoon argues, this is a strategy "in a larger campaign to shock and amuse an audience familiar, on the one hand, with the conventions of earlier love elegy and, on the other, with the demands of Augustan moral legislation and imperial expansion" ("The Bed as Battlefield," 293).

4. See Mary-Kay Gamel, "*Non Sine Caede.*"

Notes to Pages 68–76

5. Leslie Cahoon, "Let the Muse Sing On," 200. Cahoon points up the educative value of being confronted with "the breakdown of real love" in Ovid. Her comments are worth citing; "For myself and for my students, I have found such dark visions the most resonant and the most productive. For the culturally estranged, the shock of evil and the confrontation with evil bring more reformation than do the loftiest pieties" (201). In addition, Amy Richlin, in "Hijacking the Palladion," points up the politics of gender in Ovid which can be *neither* easily ignored *nor* easily understood; "Their [Ovid's poems] combination of stylistic brilliance with violent content, especially violence against women, I find fascinating but repellent. . . . I think Ovid's texts take pleasure in violence" (179).

6. Amy Richlin, "Reading Ovid's Rapes," 178.

7. In "Rape and Rape Victims in the *Metamorphoses*," Leo Curran takes the view that although Ovid "may not always have shown great respect for women as a sex, his fascination with them led him to an insight . . . almost unique in ancient literature" (283).

8. Alison Keith, *Amores,* 329.

9. See Leslie Cahoon's analysis of the imagery of war and conquest in "The Bed as Battlefield."

10. Alison Keith, "*Corpus Eroticum,*" 31.

11. See Maria Wyke's discussion of Corinna's function as a "signifier of erotic (specifically Ovidian) discourse," as a narrative subject rather than as a girlfriend in "Reading Female Flesh." See also Alison Keith, "*Corpus Eroticum.*"

12. In "A Program for Betrayal," Leslie Cahoon writes, "the Ovidian lover burns with passion, perhaps for elegy itself, perhaps for the idea of love, perhaps for women in general, or perhaps for all attractive *pueri* and *puellae,* but not for any individual beloved" (29).

13. See Alison Keith's discussion of Ovid's indebtedness to and awareness of Propertius in "*Amores* 1.1," especially 336–43.

14. See the discussion of Alison Keith, "*Amores* 1.1"; "it may not be too fanciful to see in *emodulanda* a punning reference to the subject of the poem, the poet's choice of *modus.*"

15. Leslie Cahoon, "The Bed as Battlefield," 295.

16. See Leo Curran, "*Desultores amoris*"; H. Akbar Khan, "*Ovidius Furens*"; Katherine Olstein, "*Amores* 1.3."

17. Mary Ann Doane, *The Desire to Desire,* 6.

18. Teresa de Lauretis, *Technologies of Gender,* 44.

19. In "The Bed as Battlefield," Leslie Cahoon makes the crucial observation that in the *Amores,* "the theme of erotic warfare is not merely a witty exercise, but also an exposé of the competitive, violent, and destructive nature of *amor*" (294).

20. Leo Curran's interpretation of this is well put: "The identification of himself (Ovid) with Jupiter, jumping from love affair to love affair, is a curious choice for a lover who advertises himself as a model of fidelity and who declared 'non mihi mille placent, non sum desultor amoris' (1.15)" ("*Desultores amoris,*" 48).

21. For helpful insights on subjectivity and language in psychoanalysis, see Kaja Silverman, *The Subject of Semiotics.* For illuminating discussions of the implications of

Freudian and Lacanian theories about how female subjectivity is structured negatively "in relation to the phallus," see Teresa de Lauretis, *The Technology of Gender*.

22. See Page duBois' analysis of metaphors used for the female body in ancient culture in *Sowing the Body*.

23. Mary-Kay Gamel, "*Non Sine Caede*," 197. For a provocative discussion on the woman as *materia* in Roman elegy, particularly on Propertian elegy, see Maria Wyke, "Written Women."

24. See Stephen Hinds' discussion of *Amores* 1.5 in "Generalising about Ovid." In this poem, Hinds envisions Corinna as having "the attributes of a goddess" and regards her entry into the *Amores* as "charged with something of the numinousness of epiphany" (11). My argument here will attempt to refute this view.

25. See, for example, L. P. Wilkinson, *Ovid Recalled*, 53.

26. See R. O. A. M. Lyne for this view in *The Latin Love Poets*, especially 259–64.

27. Alison Keith, "*Corpus Eroticum*," 29.

28. Stephen Hinds, "Generalising about Ovid," 11.

29. Ibid., 9.

30. On this point, see W. S. M. Nicoll, "Ovid, *Amores* 1.5," 43; and Stephen Hinds, "Generalising about Ovid," 10.

31. W. S. M. Nicoll, "Ovid, *Amores* 1.5," 43.

32. Some notable examples from the *Aeneid* are the appearance of Hector's ghost (II.268 ff.), Aeneas' vision of the Penates (III.147 ff.), his vision of the nymphs who were once his ships (X.215 ff.), and Allecto's visits to Amata and Turnus (VII.341 ff. and 414 ff.).

33. I. M. Le M. Du Quesnay, "The *Amores*," 31.

34. Stephen Hinds, "Generalising about Ovid," 10. Likewise, W. S. M. Nichols comments, "With *ecce, Corinna venit* Ovid again reverts to a familiar feature of the Virgilian apparition—the dramatic epiphany introduced by *ecce*" ("Ovid, *Amores* 1.5," 46).

35. See for example, Plutarch, *Moralia*, volumes III, IV, and V, translated by F. C. Barrett (Loeb Classical Library). See also Diodorus of Sicily, *Library of History*, Book II.

36. I thank W. S. Anderson for bringing this to my attention. Alternatively, if we read *thalamos* to mean *bridal rooms*, then it is possible that Ovid wants to focus on the image of Semiramis as a virgin bride. Seen in this way, the allusion to Semiramis may show the way in which the poetic narrator refashions myth to suit his amatory purposes in much the same way as he fashions the *puella* to mirror his own desires. In that case, the images of Semiramis and Lais would represent the binary oppositions of goddess/queen and whore.

37. Diodorus recounts that after Semiramis brought her public works to completion, as the Queen of Babylon, she went to the city of Media and passed a great deal of time there, "enjoying every form of indulgence; and though she was unwilling to contract a formal marriage, for fear lest someday she might be deprived of her sovereignty, yet selecting for herself those of the soldiers outstanding for comeliness, she made love to them, then slew every one of them who had shared her bed" (in Diodorus, *Library of History*, 18–19).

38. Alison Keith, "*Corpus Eroticum*," 30.

39. Stephen Hinds, "Generalising about Ovid," 10–11.

40. In "Diana Described," see Nancy Vickers' discussion of Petrarch's "poetics of fragmentation" in which he portrays his beloved Laura "as a part or parts of a woman." The unity of the speaker's self, Vickers argues, depends on the repetition of the woman's dismembered image. Vickers' analysis is very useful for understanding Ovid's description of Corinna in this poem.

41. Stephen Keith, "*Corpus Eroticum*," 31.

42. See Peter Green's notes on *Amores* 1.5 in his translation of the *Amores* in *Ovid, the Erotic Poems*, 273.

43. See Laura Mulvey's highly influential essay, "Visual Pleasure and Narrative Cinema."

44. Ibid., 436.

45. I thank Kate Toll for bringing this to my attention.

46. Nancy Vickers, "Diana Described," 102.

47. See Margaret Williamson's discussion of the female lover's "objectifying gaze" in Sappho 31 in "Sappho and the Other Woman."

48. See Yopie Prins, "Sappho's Afterlife in Translation." Prins traces various English translations of Sappho 31 from the seventeenth century to the present and specifically examines the representations of Sappho's broken tongue (the central image of fragmentation in the poem).

49. See Eva Stehle (Stigers), "Sappho's Gaze," 108.

50. Laura Mulvey writes, "Hence the look, pleasurable in form, can be threatening in content, and it is woman as representation/image that crystallizes this paradox" ("Visual Pleasure," 436).

51. For example, in *Ovid, the Erotic Poems* (273), Peter Green calls *Amores* 1.5 "among the most charming and direct of Ovid's erotic poems."

52. See Hermann Fränkel, *Ovid*, 18; Georg Luck, *The Latin Love Elegy*, 149; and L. P. Wilkinson, *Ovid Recalled*, 50.

53. Peter Connor, "His Dupes and Accomplices"; and Douglass Parker, "The Ovidian Coda."

54. In the *Aeneid*, Virgil often uses the word *furor* to denote a kind of divine wrath which, although violent and destructive, also leads to the establishment of Rome in Italy. In that context, perhaps Ovid's use of *furor* here might be construed as ironic because Virgilian *furor* is, in part, a means of asserting (male) imperialistic dominance. The use of *vesana* recalls Catullus 7 where Catullus associates *vesana* with an erotic obsession he celebrates rather than denounces.

55. Leo Curran, "Rape and Rape Victims," 84.

56. For an analysis of how Ovid's Pygmalion story in the *Metamorphoses* "is precisely the story of the elegist," see A. R. Sharrock, "Womanufacture."

57. Ibid., 40.

58. Teresa de Lauretis, *Technologies of Gender*, 43–44.

59. H. Akbar Khan, "*Ovidius Furens*," 894.

CHAPTER FIVE. Sexual Politics in Ovid's *Amores*

Brief portions of this chapter appeared in my article "Sexual Politics in Ovid's Amores." *Classical Philology* 89, no. 4 (1994): 344–51. Copyright 1994 by The University of Chicago. All rights reserved.

  1. See John T. Davis, *Fictus Adulter*. Davis offers an insightful and detailed analysis of the *amator*'s role playing and deception in the *Amores;* see, especially, Chapter 3, "The Protean Lover: Ovid the Poseur," 57–100.
  2. Unlike Ovid, Catullus separates the public world of the marketplace and the private world of love; for illustrations of this, see my discussion of Poems 5 and 7 in Chapter 2.
  3. Julie Hemker, "Rape and the Founding of Rome," 45.
  4. Mary-Kay Gamel, "*Non Sine Caede*," 185.
  5. Katherine Olstein, "*Amores* 1.3 and Duplicity."
  6. Leslie Cahoon, "The Bed as Battlefield." Cahoon's essay is an astute analysis of the connections in the *Amores* between love and conquest. In particular, Cahoon points out that the *Amores* are an exposé of the competitive and violent nature of *amor,* "an exposé that calls into question fundamental Roman attitudes in both the public and private spheres" (6).
  7. In *The History of Sexuality* Michel Foucault's insistence on the necessity of reading sexuality in relation to the larger social order has had a profound influence on scholars investigating the nature of sexuality and its relation to structures and institutions of power. As Marilyn Skinner puts it, "Sexual conduct . . . is infused with meanings that resonate to a profound degree with other, nominally ungendered, arrangements, most notably prestige and power systems" ("*Ego Mulier,*" 108).
  8. Teresa De Lauretis, *Technologies of Gender*, 5. De Lauretis argues that the "assymetry that characterizes all gender systems" is inextricably linked to social inequality.
  9. See Gayle Rubin's important essay, "The Traffic in Women," 158.
  10. See Teresa de Lauretis, *Technologies of Gender*, 8. "The 'doubled' perspective of contemporary feminist analysis . . . is one in which we can see the two orders, the sexual and the economic, operate together." See also Elaine Showalter, "Introduction: The Rise of Gender," "gender is not only a question of *difference,* which assumes that the sexes are separate and equal; but of *power,* since in looking at the history of gender relations, we find sexual asymmetry, inequality, and male dominance in every known society" (4).
  11. On this point, see Leslie Cahoon, Ovid and His *Praecepta Amoris,* 78–120.
  12. See Kenneth Quinn, *Latin Explorations,* particular the chapter "Ovid the Poseur," 266–73.
  13. Leslie Cahoon, Ovid and His *Praecepta Amoris,* 97–98.
  14. Both Leslie Cahoon, "A Program for Betrayal," and John T. Davis, *Fictus Adulter,* have important insights about the *amator*'s inconsistent strategies for seduction.
  15. Luce Irigaray, "This Sex Which Is Not One." Irigaray's work has been extremely influential in articulating important ideas about the question of woman's *essence* and of a female sexuality.

16. In *The Elementary Structures of Kinship*, Claude Lévi-Strauss analyzes the origin and nature of human society, giving particular importance to the "gift" and the incest taboo. These two elements, as Gayle Rubin points out, add up to "his concept of the exchange of women" (171). In this context, see also Marcel Mauss, *The Gift* (first published in 1954 as *The Gift: Forms and Functions of Exchange in Archaic Societies*). It is Mauss who first discussed the extent to which giving and receiving gifts dominate social interactions in primitive societies.

17. Gayle Rubin, "The Traffic in Women," 174.

18. Luce Irigaray writes, "The trade that organizes patriarchal societies takes place exclusively among men" (from "This Sex Which Is Not One," *New French Feminisms*, 107).

19. See Nancy Sorkin Rabinowitz's discussion of the Lévi-Strauss model of the exchange in women in *Anxiety Veiled*, especially 15–22. Rabinowitz points out that Lévi-Strauss not only defines the triangle among man, woman, and group but also alludes to the "romantic triangle constituted by male rivals for a woman" (17). Thus, as Rabinowitz observes, the triangle among "the man who gives, the man who receives, and the woman . . . highlights a crucial consequence of the traffic in women": that the exchange of women "creates a world in which relationships between men are formed and validated by women, who in some sense are then just a link—but, given normative heterosexuality, a necessary one" (17–18).

20. Luce Irigaray's words seem apt in this context, "For woman is traditionally a use-value for man, an exchange value among men; in other words, a commodity. . . . . Woman is never anything but the locus of a more or less competitive exchange between two men" ("This Sex Which Is Not One," 355).

21. Gayle Rubin, "The Traffic in Women," 175.

22. There is much debate concerning the degree of power male guardians still had over women in Augustan society. For discussions of Roman marriage, see Eva Cantarella, *Pandora's Daughters*, especially Chapters 9 and 10; Elaine Fantham et al., eds., *Women in the Classical World*, especially Chapters 10 and 11; Judith Hallett, *Fathers and Daughters in Roman Society*; Sarah B. Pomeroy, *Goddesses, Whores, Wives, and Slaves*, especially 149–63; and Susan Treggiari, *Roman Marriage*.

23. See Maria Wyke's studies of how elegiac woman, in Propertius' texts, is subordinated to her role as *materia* for the poet's literary productions ("Written Women").

Bibliography

Adams, J. N. *The Latin Sexual Vocabulary*. London: Duckworth Press, 1982.
Adler, Eve. *Catullan Self-Revelation*. New York: Arno Press, 1981.
Allen, A. W. "*Sunt Qui Propertium Malint.*" In *Critical Essays on Roman Literature*, edited by J. P. Sullivan, 107–48. Cambridge: Harvard University Press, 1962.
Ancona, Ronnie. "The Subterfuge of Reason: Horace, *Odes* 1.23, and the Construction of Male Desire." *Helios* 19 (1989): 49–55.
Archer, Léonie, Susan Fischler, and Maria Wyke, eds. *Women in Ancient Societies*. New York: Routledge, 1994.
Arthur, Marylin. "Early Greece: The Origins of the Western Attitude toward Women." In *Women in the Ancient World: The Arethusa Papers*, edited by John Peradotto and J. P. Sullivan, 7–58. Albany, N.Y.: State University of New York Press, 1984.
Baker, R. J. "Beauty and the Beast in Propertius 1.3." In *Studies in Latin Literature and Roman History*, vol. 2, edited by Carl Deroux, 245–58. Brussels: Latomus, 1980.
Barsby, J. A. "Rhythmical Factors in Catullus 72, 75, and 76." *Phoenix* 29 (1975): 83–88.
Barthes, Roland. *A Lover's Discourse*. New York: Hill and Wang, 1978.
Bartky, Sandra Lee. *Femininity and Domination*. New York: Routledge, 1990.
Bassi, Karen. "Desired Silence: *Amor* and *Mors* in Tibullus 1.1." *Syllecta Classica* (1994).
Benjamin, Jessica. *The Bonds of Love, Psychoanalysis, Feminism, and the Problem of Domination*. New York: Pantheon, 1988.
Benveniste, Emile. *Problems in General Linguistics*. Miami, Fla.: University of Miami Press, 1977.
Blodgett, E. D., and Rosemary Nielsen. "Mask and Figure in Catullus, Carmen 11." *Revue Belge de Philologie et Histoire* 64 (1986): 22–31.
Bright, D. F. "*Non Bona Dicta:* Catullus' Poetry of Separation." *Quaderni Urbinati di cultura classica* 21 (1976): 105–19.
Butler, Judith. *Gender Trouble*. New York: Routledge, 1990.
———. *Bodies That Matter*. New York: Routledge, 1993.
Cahoon, Leslie. "Ovid and His *Praecepta Amoris*." Ph.D. diss., University of California, Berkeley, 1981.

———. "A Program for Betrayal: Ovidian *Nequitia* in the *Amores.*" *Helios* 12 (1985): 29–39.

———. "The Bed as Battlefield: Erotic Conquest and Military Metaphor in Ovid's *Amores.*" *Transactions of the American Philological Association* 118 (1988): 293–307.

———. "Let the Muse Sing On: Poetry, Criticism, Feminism, and the Case of Ovid." *Helios* 17 (1990): 197–211.

Cameron, Averil, and Amelie Kuhrt, eds. *Images of Women in Antiquity.* Detroit: Wayne State University Press, 1983.

Cantarella, Eva. *Pandora's Daughters: The Role and Status of Women in Greek and Roman Antiquity,* translated by Maureen B. Fant. Baltimore: Johns Hopkins University Press, 1987.

Carson, Anne. *Eros the Bittersweet.* Princeton: Princeton University Press, 1986.

Commager, Steele. "Notes on Some Poems of Catullus." *Harvard Studies in Classical Philology* (1965): 83–110.

Connor, Peter. "Catullus 8: The Lover's Conflict." *Antichthon* 8 (1974): 93–96.

———. "His Dupes and Accomplices: Ovid the Illusionist in the *Amores.*" *Ramus* 3 (1974): 18–40.

Copley, Frank. "*Servitium Amoris* in the Roman Elegists." *Transactions of the American Philological Association* 78 (1947): 285–300.

———. "Emotional Conflict and Its Significance in the Lesbia Poems of Catullus." *American Journal of Philology* 70 (1949): 22–40.

Culham, Phyllis. "Ten Years after Pomeroy: Studies of the Image and Reality of Women in Antiquity." *Helios* 13 (1987): 9–30.

———. "Decentering the Text: The Case of Ovid." *Helios* 17 (1990): 161–70.

Curran, Leo. "*Desultores amoris:* Ovid *Amores* 1.3." *Classical Philology* 61 (1966): 47–49.

———. "Vision and Reality in Propertius 1.3." *Yale Classical Studies* 19 (1966): 189–207.

———. "Poetic Counterpoint: Catullus, 72." *American Journal of Philology* 92 (1971): 196–201.

———. "Rape and Rape Victims in the *Metamorphoses.*" In *Women in the Ancient World: The Arethusa Papers,* edited by John Peradotto and J. P. Sullivan, 263–86. Albany, N.Y.: State University of New York Press, 1984.

Davis, John T. "Poetic Counterpoint: Catullus 72." *American Journal of Philology* 92 (1971): 196–201.

———. "*Risit Amor:* Aspects of Literary Burlesque in Ovid's *Amores.*" *Aufsteig und Niedergang Der Romischen Welt* II (1981): 2460–2506.

———. *Fictus Adulter: Poet as Actor in the Amores.* Amsterdam: Gieben, 1990.

Day, A. A. *The Origins of Latin Love Elegy.* Oxford: Oxford University Press, 1938.

de Lauretis, Teresa. *Technologies of Gender.* Bloomington, Ind.: Indiana University Press, 1987.

Diodorus of Sicily. *Library of History,* Book II. In *The Antiquities of Asia,* translated and edited by Edwin Murphy. New Brunswick, N.J.: Transaction Publishers, 1989.

Doane, Mary Ann. *The Desire to Desire.* Bloomington, Ind.: Indiana University Press, 1987.

duBois, Page. *Sowing the Body: Psychoanalysis and Ancient Representations of Women.* Chicago: University of Chicago Press, 1988.

Dunn, F. M. "The Lover Reflected in the *Exemplum:* A Study of Propertius 1.3 and 2.6." *Illinois Classical Studies* 10 (1985): 233–59.

Du Quesnay, I. M. Le M. "The *Amores.*" In *Ovid,* edited by J. W. Binns, 1–48. London: Routledge, 1973.

Dyson, M. "Catullus 8 and 76." *Classical Quarterly* 23 (1973): 127–43.

Edwards, Catharine. *The Politics of Immorality in Ancient Rome.* Cambridge: Cambridge University Press, 1993.

Elder, J. P. "Notes on Some Conscious and Unconscious Elements in Catullus' Poetry." *Harvard Studies in Classical Philology* 60 (1951): 101–36.

Elliott, Alison Goddard. "Ovid and the Critics." *Helios* 11 (1985): 9–19.

Fantham, Elaine, Helene Foley, Natalie Kampen, Sarah Pomeroy, and H. Alan Shapiro, eds. *Women in the Classical World.* Oxford: Oxford University Press, 1994.

Faraone, Christopher. "Sex and Power: Male-Targeting Aphrodisiacs in the Greek Magical Tradition." *Helios* 19 (1992): 92–103.

———. "The Wheel, the Whip, and Other Implements of Torture: Erotic Magic in Pindar *Pythian* 4.213–19." *Classical Journal* 89 (1993): 1–19.

Faraone, C. A., and D. Obbink, eds. *Magika Hiera: Ancient Greek Magic and Religion.* Oxford: Oxford University Press, 1991.

Fitzgerald, William. *Catullan Provocations.* Berkeley: University of California Press, 1995.

Flax, Jane. "Postmodernism and Gender Relations in Feminist Theory." *Signs* 12 (1986): 621–43.

Foley, Helene, ed. *Reflections of Women in Antiquity.* New York: Gordon and Breach, 1981.

Forsyth, P. Y. "Catullus: The Mythic Persona." *Latomus* 35 (1976): 555–66.

———. "Thematic Unity of Catullus 11." *Classical World* 84 (1991): 457–64.

Foucault, Michel. *The History of Sexuality,* vols. 1, 2, and 3. New York: Vintage, 1980, 1986, 1988.

Fraenkel, Eduard. "*Vesper Adest.*" *Journal of Roman Studies* (1955): 6.

———. "Two Poems of Catullus." *Journal of Roman Studies* 51 (1961): 46–53.

Fränkel, Hermann. *Ovid, A Poet Between Two Worlds.* Berkeley: University of California Press, 1945.

Fredricksmeyer, Ernst. "The Beginning and the End of Catullus' *Longus Amor.*" *Symbolae Osloenses* 58 (1983): 63–88.

———. "Method and Interpretation: Catullus 11." *Helios* 20 (1993): 89–105.

Freis, Richard. "Form and Thought in Catullus 76." *Agon* 1 (1968): 39–58.

Fuss, Diana. *Essentially Speaking: Feminism, Nature, and Difference.* New York: Routledge, 1989.

Gamel, Mary-Kay. "Introduction." *Helios* 12 (1985): 3–7.

———. "*Non Sine Caede:* Abortion Politics and Poetics in Ovid's *Amores.*" *Helios* 16 (1989): 183–206.

———. "Reading Reality." *Helios* 17 (1990): 171–74.

Gardner, Jane F. *Women in Roman Law and Society.* Bloomington, Ind.: Indiana University Press, 1986.

Gold, Barbara. " 'But Ariadne Was Never There in the First Place': Finding the Female in Roman Poetry." In *Feminist Theory and the Classics,* edited by Nancy Sorkin Rabinowitz and Amy Richlin, 75–101. New York: Routledge, 1993.

Green, Peter. *Ovid, the Erotic Poems.* New York: Penguin, 1982.
Greene, Ellen. "Sexual Politics in Ovid's *Amores:* 3.4, 3.8, and 3.12." *Classical Philology* 89 (1994): 344–51.
———. "The Catullan *Ego:* Fragmentation and the Erotic Self." *American Journal of Philology* 116 (1995): 77–94.
———. "Elegiac Woman: Fantasy, *Materia,* and Male Desire in Propertius 1.3 and 1.11." *American Journal of Philology* 116 (1995): 303–18.
Griffin, Jasper. *Latin Poets and Roman Life.* Chapel Hill, N.C.: University of North Carolina Press, 1986.
Hallett, Judith. *Fathers and Daughters in Roman Society: Women in the Elite Family.* Princeton: Princeton University Press, 1984.
———. "The Role of Women in Roman Elegy: Counter-Cultural Feminism." In *Women in the Ancient World,* edited by John Peradotto and J. P. Sullivan, 241–62. Albany, N.Y.: State University of New York Press, 1984.
———. "Contextualizing the Text: The Journey to Ovid." *Helios* 17 (1990): 187–95.
Harmon, Daniel. "Catullus 72.3–4." *Classical Journal* 65 (1970): 321–22.
———. "Myth and Fantasy in Propertius 1.3." *Transactions of the American Philological Association* 104 (1974): 151–65.
Havelock, Eric. *The Lyric Genius of Catullus.* Oxford: Oxford University Press, 1939.
Hemker, Julie. "Rape and the Founding of Rome." *Helios* 12 (1985): 41–47.
Hinds, Stephen. "Generalising about Ovid." In *The Imperial Muse: Ramus Essays on Roman Literature of the Empire,* edited by A. J. Boyle, 4–31. Victoria, Australia, 1988.
Irigaray, Luce. "This Sex Which Is Not One." In *Feminisms,* edited by Robyn Warhol and Diane Herndl, 350–56. New Brunswick, N.J.: Rutgers University Press, 1991.
Janan, Micaela. *"When the Lamp Is Shattered": Desire and Narrative in Catullus.* Carbondale, Ill.: Southern Illinois University Press, 1994.
Johnson, W. R. *The Idea of Lyric.* Berkeley: University of California Press, 1982.
———. "Ringing Down the Curtain on Love." *Helios* 11 (1985): 21–29.
Kaplan, E. Ann. "Is the Gaze Male?" In *Powers of Desire,* edited by A. Snitow, 309–27. New York: Monthly Review Press, 1983.
Keith, Alison. "*Amores* 1.1: Propertius and the Ovidian Programme." In *Collection Latomus,* edited by Carl Deroux, 327–44. Brussels: Latomus, 1992.
———. "*Corpus Eroticum:* Elegiac Poetics and Elegiac *Puellae* in Ovid's *Amores.*" *Classical World* 88 (1994): 27–40.
Kennedy, Duncan F. *The Arts of Love: Five Studies in the Discourse of Roman Love Elegy.* Cambridge: Cambridge University Press, 1993.
Keuls, Eva. "The Feminist View of the Past: A Comment on the 'Decentering' of the Poems of Ovid." *Helios* 17 (1990): 221–24.
Khan, H. Akbar. "*Ovidius Furens:* A Revaluation of *Amores* 1.7." *Latomus* 25 (1966): 880–94.
King, J. K. "Propertius' Programmatic Poetry and the Unity of the *Monobiblos.*" *Classical Journal* 71 (1975): 108–24.
Kinsey, T. E. "Catullus 11." *Latomus* 24 (1965): 537–44.
Konstan, David. "Two Kinds of Love in Catullus." *Classical Journal* 68 (1972): 102–6.
Lee, A. G. "*Tenerorum Lusor Amorum.*" In *Critical Essays on Roman Literature,* edited by J. P. Sullivan, 149–80. Cambridge: Harvard University Press, 1962.

Lefkowitz, Mary R., and Maureen Fant, eds. *Women's Life in Greece and Rome.* Baltimore: Johns Hopkins University Press, 1982.

Lévi-Strauss, Claude. *The Elementary Structures of Kinship,* translated by James Bell, John Sturmer, and Rodney Needham and edited by Rodney Needham. Boston: Beacon Press, 1966. Translation of *Les structures élémentaires de parenté,* 1949.

Lipking, Lawrence. *Abandoned Women and Poetic Tradition.* Chicago: University of Chicago Press, 1988.

Luck, Georg. *The Latin Love Elegy.* London, 1959.

———. *Arcana Mundi: Magic and the Occult in the Greek and Roman Worlds.* Baltimore: Johns Hopkins University Press, 1985.

Lyne, R. O. A. M. "Propertius and Cynthia: *Elegy* 1.3." *Proceedings of the Cambridge Philological Society* 16 (1970): 60–78.

———. "*Servitium Amoris.*" *Classical Quarterly* 29 (1979): 117–30.

———. *The Latin Love Poets.* Oxford: Oxford University Press, 1980.

Mack, Sara. *Ovid.* New Haven: Yale University Press, 1988.

Marks, Elaine, and Isabelle de Courtivron, eds. *New French Feminisms.* New York: Schocken, 1981.

Martin, Charles. *The Poems of Catullus.* New Haven: Yale University Press, 1992.

Mauss, Marcel. *The Gift,* translated by Ian Cunnison. New York: Norton, 1967. Translation of *Essai sur le don,* 1925.

McKie, David. "The Horrible and Ultimate Britons: Catullus 11." *Proceedings of the Cambridge Philological Society* 210 (1984): 74–78.

Miller, Paul Allen. "Catullus, C. 70: A Poem and Its Hypothesis." *Helios* 15–16 (1988): 127–32.

———. *Lyric Texts and Lyric Consciousness: The Birth of a Genre from Archaic Greece to Augustan Rome.* New York: Routledge, 1994.

Moi, Toril. *Sexual/Textual Politics: Feminist Literary Theory.* New York: Routledge, 1985.

Mulroy, David. "An Interpretation of Catullus 11." *Classical World* 71 (1977): 82–93.

Mulvey, Laura. "Visual Pleasure and Narrative Cinema." In *Feminisms,* edited by Robyn Warhol and Diane Price Herndl, 432–42. New Brunswick, N.J.: Rutgers University Press, 1991.

Myerowitz, Molly. *Ovid's Games of Love.* Detroit: Wayne State University Press, 1985.

Newman, John. *Roman Catullus and the Modification of the Alexandrian Sensibility.* Hildesheim, Germany: Weidmann Press, 1990.

Nicoll, W. S. M. "Ovid, *Amores* 1.5." *Mnemosyne* 30 (1977): 40–48.

Olstein, Katherine. "*Amores* 1.3 and Duplicity as a Way of Love." *Transactions of the American Philological Association* 105 (1975): 241–57.

Parker, Douglass. "The Ovidian Coda." *Arion* 8 (1969): 80–97.

Peradotto, John, and J. P. Sullivan, eds. *Women in the Ancient World: The Arethusa Papers.* Albany, N.Y.: State University of New York Press, 1984.

Plumwood, Val. "Women, Humanity, and Nature." In *Socialism, Feminism, and Philosophy,* edited by Sean Sayers, 211–34. New York: Routledge, 1990.

Plutarch. *Moralia,* vols. III, IV, and V. Translated by F. C. Barrett. Cambridge: Harvard University Press, 1972 (originally published in 1936).

Pomeroy, Sarah B. *Goddesses, Whores, Wives, and Slaves: Women in Classical Antiquity.* New York: Schocken, 1975.

———, ed. *Women's History and Ancient History*. Chapel Hill, N.C.: University of North Carolina Press, 1991.
Prins, Yopie. "Sappho's Afterlife in Translation." In *Re-Reading Sappho: Reception and Transmission*, edited by Ellen Greene, 36–67. Berkeley: University of California Press, 1997.
Putnam, Michael, ed. "Catullus 11: The Ironies of Integrity." In *Essays on Latin Lyric, Elegy, and Epic*, 13–29. Princeton: Princeton University Press, 1982.
Quinn, Kenneth. *The Catullan Revolution*. Carlton, Australia: Melbourne University Press, 1959.
———. *Latin Explorations*. London: Routledge, 1963.
———. *Catullus: The Poems*. London: Macmillan, 1970.
———. *Approaches to Catullus*. New York: Barnes and Noble, 1972.
Rabinowitz, Nancy Sorkin. *Anxiety Veiled: Euripides and the Traffic in Women*. Ithaca: Cornell University Press, 1993.
Rabinowitz, Nancy Sorkin, and Amy Richlin, eds. *Feminist Theory and the Classics*. New York: Routledge, 1993.
Richardson, L. "*Furi et Aureli, Comites Catulli*." *Classical Philology* 58 (1963): 93–106.
Richlin, Amy. "Hijacking the Palladion." *Helios* 17 (1990): 175–85.
———. "Reading Ovid's Rapes." In *Pornography and Representation in Greece and Rome*, edited by Amy Richlin, 158–79. Oxford: Oxford University Press, 1992.
Ross, David. *Style and Tradition in Catullus*. Cambridge: Harvard University Press, 1969.
———. *Backgrounds to Augustan Poetry: Gallus, Elegy, and Rome*. Cambridge: Cambridge University Press, 1975.
Rowland, R. L. "*Miser Catulle:* An Interpretation of the Eighth Poem of Catullus." *Greece and Rome* 13 (1966): 15–21.
Rubin, Gayle. "The Traffic in Women: Notes on the 'Political Economy' of Sex." In *Toward an Anthropology of Women*, edited by Rayna Reiter, 157–210. New York: Monthly Review Press, 1975.
Rubino, Carl. "The Erotic World of Catullus." *Classical World* 68 (1975): 289–99.
Scafuro, Adele, and Eva Stehle, eds. "Studies on Roman Women." *Helios* 16 (1989): 1–2.
Scott, R. T. "On Catullus 11." *Classical Philology* 78 (1983): 39–42.
Sedgwick, Eve Kosofsky. *Between Men: English Literature and Male Homosocial Desire*. New York: Columbia University Press, 1985.
Segal, Charles. "Catullus 5 and 7: A Study in Complementarities." *American Journal of Philology* 89 (1968): 284–301.
———. "Ovid: Metamorphosis, Hero, Poet." *Helios* 12 (1985): 49–64.
Selden, Daniel. "*Ceveat lector:* Catullus and the Rhetoric of Performance." In *Innovations in Antiquity*, edited by Daniel Selden and Ralph Hexter, 461–512. New York: Routledge, 1992.
Sharrock, A. R. "Womanufacture." *Journal of Roman Studies* 81 (1991): 36–49.
Showalter, Elaine. "Introduction: The Rise of Gender." In *Speaking of Gender*, edited by Elaine Showalter, 1–16. New York: Routledge, 1989.
Silverman, Kaja. *The Subject of Semiotics*. New York: Oxford University Press, 1983.
Skinner, Marilyn. "Catullus 8: The Comic *amator* as *eiron*." *Classical Journal* 66 (1971): 298–305.

———. "Parasites and Strange Bedfellows: A Study in Catullus' Political Imagery." *Ramus* 8 (1980): 137–52.
———. "Disease Imagery in Catullus 76.17–26." *Classical Philology* 82 (1987): 230–33.
———. "*Ut Decuit Cinaediorem:* Power, Gender, and Urbanity in Catullus 10." *Helios* 16 (1989): 7–23.
———. "*Ego Mulier:* The Construction of Male Sexuality in Catullus." *Helios* 20 (1993): 107–30.
———, ed. "Rescuing Creusa: New Methodological Approaches to Women in Antiquity." *Helios* 13 (1986).
Spelman, Elizabeth V. *Inessential Woman: Problems of Exclusion in Feminist Thought.* Boston: Beacon Press, 1988.
Stahl, Hans-Peter. *Propertius: Love and War: Individual and State under Augustus.* Berkeley: University of California Press, 1985.
Stehle (Stigers), Eva. "Retreat from the Male: Catullus 62 and Sappho's Erotic Flowers." *Ramus* 6 (1977): 83–102.
———. "Sappho's Gaze: Fantasies of a Goddess and a Young Man." *differences* 2 (1990): 88–125.
Sweet, David. "Catullus 11: A Study in Perspective." *Latomus* 46 (1987): 510–26.
Tracy, Valerie. "Ovid's Self-Portrait in the *Amores.*" *Helios* 6 (1978): 57–62.
Treggiari, Susan. *Roman Marriage.* Oxford: Oxford University Press, 1991.
Veyne, Paul. *Roman Erotic Elegy.* Chicago: University of Chicago Press, 1988.
Vickers, Nancy. "Diana Described: Scattered Women and Scattered Rhyme." In *Writing and Sexual Difference,* edited by Elizabeth Abel, 95–109. Chicago: University of Chicago Press, 1980.
Virgil. The *Aeneid,* translated by Allen Mandelbaum. New York: Bantam, 1981.
Warden, John. *Fallax Opus: Poet and Reader in the Elegies of Propertius.* Toronto: University of Toronto Press, 1980.
Wilkinson, L. P. *Ovid Recalled.* Cambridge: Cambridge University Press, 1955.
Williamson, Margaret. "Sappho and the Other Woman." In *Reading Sappho: Contemporary Approaches,* edited by Ellen Greene, 248–64. Berkeley: University of California Press, 1997.
Winkler, John J. *The Constraints of Desire: The Anthropology of Sex and Gender in Ancient Greece.* New York: Routledge, 1990.
Wiseman, T. P. *Catullus and His World: A Reappraisal.* Oxford: Oxford University Press, 1985.
Wyke, Maria. "Written Women: Propertius' *Scripta Puella.*" *Journal of Roman Studies* 77 (1987): 47–61.
———. "Mistress and Metaphor in Augustan Elegy." *Helios* 16 (1989): 25–47.
———. "Reading Female Flesh: *Amores* 3.1." In *History as Text,* edited by Averil Cameron, 113–43. Chapel Hill, N.C.: University of North Carolina Press, 1990.
Yardley, J. C. 1978. "Catullus 11.7–8." *Liverpool Classical Monthly* 3 (1978): 143.
———. "Catullus 11: The End of a Friendship." *Symbolae Osloenses* 56 (1981): 63–69.

Index

Abandonment: gender-specific reaction to, 6–7; as mask, 112; as moral degradation, 9, 11
Adler, Eve: on Catullan devaluation of male comrades, 30; on Catullan passivity, 6; on Catullan self-division, 1–2, 29
Adultery. *See* Infidelity
Aeneid: apparitions in, 79; death as beauty in, 35; Ovidian comparison with, 70
Ajax, 85–86
Amores. *See* Ovidian *Amores*
Ancona, Ronnie, xii, 115
Andromeda, 56
Aphrodite, 87–88
Argonautica, 44
Argus, 57
Ariadne, 56, 86–87
Atalanta and Milanion, 42–44, 86–87
Aurelius, 26–27, 29–30, 32

Bacchus, 56
Baiae, 60–62, 65–66
Barthes, Roland: on divided self, 2; on gendered reaction to abandonment, 6–7; on time discontinuity, 5
Benjamin, Jessica, 51, 120

Brutality toward women, in Ovidian poems, xv, 68, 88, 89, 94
Butler, Judith, 25

Caesar imagery in Lesbia poems, 26–28, 31–36
Cahoon, Leslie, 99
Cassandra, 86
Catullan lover: as adversary of Lesbia and mercantile role, 20; antimasculine ideal of, xiv; appeal to gods by, 12–13, 15–16; castration of, 33; directed outward, 20; emotional impotence of, 5–6; enslavement of, xiii; erotic ambivalence of, 1, 33; erotic ideals of, 20; as fatherly lover, 10; feminization of, xiii, 19; fragmentation of (*see* Fragmentation of Catullan lover); hatred of Lesbia by, 11; and identification with imperial values, 31; male comrades of, 26–27, 29–30; masculine practicality of, 13; moral plane of, 25; multiple voices of (*see* Multiple voices of Catullan lover); nobility of, 25; nonconsummation by, 24; obsessional nature of, 4, 8–9, 16; passivity of, 6; in poem 5 and 7, 20–

Catullan lover (*continued*)
26; in poem 8, 2–8, 116–17; in poem 11, 26–36; in poem 72, 8–12; in poem 76, 12–17; rationality versus emotions in, 11, 13–15; rejection of Roman cultural system by, 14, 19; self-understanding of, 12; social role reversal by, xiii; vilification of Lesbia by, 26–27 (*see also* Lesbia poems)

Commercial language: in Cynthia poems, 51; in Ovidian poems, 94

Comrades, male, of Catullan lover, 26–27, 29–30, 32

Corinna poem: gaze in, 81–84; mistress as chaste and wanton in, 80–81; mistress fragmentation in, 81–84; Semiramis in, 78, 80–81. *See also* Ovidian lover

Counting, in Lesbia poems, 21–24, 118

Criticism of Latin love poets, male readings of, xii

Cupid, 71–72

Curran, Leo: on gaze, 121; on mythology, 52–55, 75, 121, 123; on Ovidian sexual violence, 68

Cynthia poems: adulteress imagery in, 60–64; apostrophes as literary strategy in, 45; commercial language in, 51; critical approaches to, 52–55; erotic magic in, 44–45, 120; female chastity in, 43; gender specificity in, 37; humor in, 45; irony in, 46, 48, 50; as lesson for other lovers, 46; male dominance in, 43; military metaphors in, 41, 43; mistress as adversary and audience in, 47; mythology in, 42–44, 53–58, 61, 121; Ponticus in, 47–49; projection in, 57; role reversal in, xv, 52, 62; romanticizing male in, 53; as showcase for poetic prowess, 37–38, 45, 49–50; sleeping Cynthia in, 55–58; symbolic order of, xv; violence in, 43; woman as helpless or dangerous in, xiv, 38; woman as nature in, 59; woman as object in, xiv–xv. *See also* Propertian lover

Danae, 100, 104

De Rerum Natura, 41

Death: beauty and, 35, 41; in Lesbia poems, 22–24, 40

Deception: by mistress, 101; by Ovidian lover, xv, 95, 99, 101, 106

Degradation, abandonment as, 9, 11

Diomedes, 87–88

duBois, Page, 25

Edwards, Catharine, 7, 9

Elegiac male lover: alternative social creed of, xiii; enslavement of, xiii; identification of, with female roles, xiii; use of political and military terminology by, xiii. *See also* Catullan lover; Ovidian lover; Propertian lover

Elegiac mistress: as commodity for exchange, xiv; as fantasy of erotic domination, xiv; subordination of to *materia*, xiii

Enjambment, Catullan departure from, 4

Erotic ambivalence of Lesbia poems, 1, 33, 116

Europa, 76

Evil, attractiveness of, 68, 123

Family bonds: exchange of women among men in, 95, 105; between father and sons, 10; in Roman society, 10–11, 64–65

Fatherly love, for Lesbia, 10

Female sexual stereotypes, 33

Feminist theory, xi–xii

Feminization of Catullan lover, xii

Field to be ploughed, woman as, 25, 76

Flax, Jane, xi

Flower and plow imagery, in Lesbia poems, 33–36

Foucault, Michel, xii

Index

Fraenkel, Eduard, 3–4
Fragmentation
— of Catullan lover: gender confounding in, 18; idealized world in, 19; inevitability of, 16; public versus private worlds in, xiv, 16, 18; rationality versus emotions in, 11, 13–15; sexually wanton woman in, xiii; time discontinuity in, 3–5, 11. *See also* Multiple voices of Catullan lover
— of Ovidian mistress, 81; gaze in, 84; perceptual ambiguity in, 79; projection in, 79–84
Fredricksmeyer, Ernst: on Catullan dichotomy of allegiances, 26–27, 29; on flower and plow imagery, 34
Freudian theory: gaze in, 51; male and female sexuality in, 73
Furius, 26–27, 29–30, 32

Gamel, Mary-Kay, 76–77
Gaze: in domination, xv, 51–52, 125; at fetishized mistress, 74, 77–84; in fragmentation of Ovidian mistress, 84; in Freudian theory, 51; gender nonspecificity of, 73–74; at sleeping mistress, 55–58, 121; as transgressive violation, 84
Gender ideology, male reading of, xii
Goddesses: gods tamed by, 41; Lesbia as, 19; woman as, 19, 117
Gods: Catullan appeal to, 12–13, 15–16; erotic feelings taught by, 41–42

Harmon, Daniel, 55–58
Horace's love poetry, male reading of, xii
Humor: in Cynthia poems, 45; in Ovidian *Amores*, 84, 91
Hypocrisy of elegiac pose, Ovid's view of, xv

Imperial conquest: Catullan lover and, 26–27; male aggression and, 73; sexual linkage with, 106. *See also* Military metaphors

Impotence, emotional, in Catullan poem 8, 5–6
Incest taboo, 127
Infidelity: of Lesbia, 32–33; of mistress in Cynthia poems, 60–64; of Ovidian lover, 75–76, 93, 102, 105; of Ovidian wife, 105; projected, 19; as Roman social foundation, 106
Io, 57, 75, 100, 104
Irony, in Cynthia poems, 46, 48, 50

Janan, Micaela, 2, 117
Jason and Medea, 97
Jupiter: infidelities of, 75–76, 107–8, 123; in Ovidian poems, 74–76, 107–8, 123; as violent and disguised, 75–76

Kaplan, E. Ann, 74, 120

Latin love poetry: male assumptions in, xii; privileging and romanticizing of male in, xii, 53
Leda, 76
Leisure, gender specificity of, xiii
Lesbia poems: adulteress imagery in, 8, 19, 32–33; appeal to gods in, 12–13, 15–16; Caesar in, 26–28, 31–36; conflicting kinds of love in, 1; death in, 22–24, 40; erotic ambivalence in, 1, 33, 116; female stereotypes in, 33; feminine materialism in, 25; flower and plow imagery in, 33–36; fragmenting in, xiv; Lesbia's experience of Catullus in, 9–10; Lesbia's lack of desire in, 19; lover as child in, 10; lyric subjectivity of, 16; multiple voices in (*see* Multiple voices of Catullan lover); nostalgia in, 4–5; numerical reckoning in, 21–24, 118; obsession in, 8–9, 16; paradoxical gender roles in, xiv; physical versus nonphysical eroticism in, 10; projection in, 19; as real world, 14; Sapphic world imagery in, 19; as showcase for poetic prowess, xiv, 20; simplistic language in, 22; time

Lesbia poems (*continued*)
    discontinuity in, 3–5, 11; transcendent union in, 20; travel imagery in, 31–32. *See also* Catullan lover
Lévi-Strauss, Claude, on exchange of women among men, 95, 103, 127
Lipking, Lawrence, 6–7
Lover as parents: in Cynthia poems, 64–65; in Lesbia poems, 10–11, 64

Maenad, 56
Magic, erotic, 44–45, 120
Male dominance: as ethic, xiii; inevitability of, 43; political control and, xvi; in Roman society, xii. *See also* Military metaphors
Mali values, Catullan rejection of, 19, 21–25, 31
Mars, 41
Masculinity: instability of, xiii; morality and, 7; Roman definition of, xii–xiii, 7; sexually wanton female as threat to, xiii; stages of, xii
Masks: in Ovidian *Amores*, 74, 90; in reaction to abandonment, 112
Materia view of woman: in Catullus, xiv, 63; in Ovid, xv, 67–68, 70; in Propertius, xiv, 37–38, 47, 52, 63
Medea and Jason, 97
Milanion and Atalanta, 42–44, 86–87
Military metaphors: in Cynthia poems, 41, 43; in Ovidian *Amores*, 70, 91, 94–95, 122
Minerva, 71
Misogyny, in Catullan poems, xiv, 20, 117
Morality: masculinity and, xii, 7; rejection as degradation of, 9, 11
Mother, mistress as, 64–65
Multiple voices
— of Catullan lover: in comparing male friends with Lesbia, 29–30; as distancing device, 116; in poem 8, 3, 6–7, 116; in poem 11, 32; in poem 72, 9–10; as reflection of divided consciousness, 2
— of Ovidian lover, 90

Mythology
— in Cynthia poems, 42–44, 53–58, 61, 121
— in Ovidian *Amores*, 85–90, 96–97, 100, 104, 107, 110, 123; as defense for hitting mistress, 85–88; divine poetic inspiration as, 71–72; heroic and dangerous journeys in, 96–99; Jupiter as violent and disguised in, 75; Jupiter infidelities in, 75–76, 107–8, 123; poetic ability to make illusion real in, 111–12; Semiramis allusions in, 78, 80–81
— in Propertian poems: Cynthia versus goddesses in, 121; erotic magic in, 44; female helplessness and captivity in, 56; idealized male in, 57; lover as soldier in, 43; poet-lover as teacher in, 42; sleeping mistress in, 53–58; suffering poet-lover in, 43–44; Thesprotus in, 61; woman as mannequin in, 58

Niobe, 110
Nostalgia, in Catullan poem 8, 4–5
Numerical reckoning, in Lesbia poems, 21–24

Obsession: in Cynthia poems, 50; in Lesbia poems, 4, 8–9, 16; in Ovidian poems, 109
Odyssey, 41
Orestes, 85–86
Ovidian *Amores:* binary portrayal of mistress in, 98–99; competitive and exploitative nature of, 68; Cupid in, 71–72; evil attractiveness in, 68, 123; gaze in, 77–84; as gendered text, 68; humor in, 91; insincerity in, 74; masks in, 74, 75–76, 90, 112; *materia* view of woman in, xv, 67–68, 70; mechanics of male power and domination in, xv, 68; military metaphors in, 70, 91, 94–95, 122; mistress as chaste and wanton in, 80–81; mockery of divine poetic

inspiration in, 71; multiple voices in, 90; mythology in, 74–76, 85–90 (*see* Mythology in Ovidian *Amores*); parody in, 84–85; as pornography, 68; as showcase for poetic prowess, 72, 98, 109; supernatural in, 77–80; wit in, 67–68, 84

Ovidian lover, xv; acceptance of Roman brutality by, xv; amatory moral indifference of, xv–xvi; in *Amores* 1.1, 68–74; in *Amores* 1.3, 74–77; in *Amores* 1.7, 84–92; in *Amores* 2.11, 95–99; in *Amores* 2.19, 3.4, and 3.8, 99–108; in *Amores* 3.12, 108–13; arousal and deception by, 101; brutality of, xv, 68, 88–89, 94; exploitation by, xv, 95, 99, 101, 106; fragmentation by, 77; infidelity of, 75–76, 93, 102, 105; lack of passion in, 72; manipulation by, 93–94; narrative contradictions of, xv; obsession in, 109; pessimism of, 93; pimping by, xv–xvi, 99, 102, 106, 109–10

Parental love for mistress, 10–11, 64–65
Penelope, 105
Penis envy, 51
Perseus and Andromeda, 56
Pimping, by Ovidian lover, xv–xvi, 99, 102, 106, 109–10
Plow and flower imagery in Lesbia poems, 33–36
Poetic showcase: Cynthia poems as, 37–38, 42; Lesbia poems as, xiv, 20; Ovidian *Amores* as, 72, 98, 109
Politics: male control of, xii; sexual dominance and, xvi; vocabulary of, xiii
Ponticus, in Cynthia poems, 47–49
Problematization of gender relations, xi
Projection: in Cynthia poems, 57; in Lesbia poems, 19
Propertian lover: appeal to witches by, 44–45; composure of, 51; in *Elegy* 1.1, 38–47; in *Elegy* 1.3, 51–59; in *Elegy* 1.7, 47–51; in *Elegy* 1.11, 59–66; enslavement of, 37, 40; hatred of chaste women, 42; manipulative strategies of, 63; *materia* view of woman, xiv, 47, 52, 63; mythological influence on, 42–44, 53–58, 61; obsession by, 50; role reversal by, xv, 66; sleeping mistress and, 55–58. *See also* Cynthia poems
Proteus, 110
Psychoanalytic theory: feminine traits in, 51
Public domain: gender ideology versus self-definition in, xiv; private domain and, in Catullan fragmentation, 16
Putnam, Michael, 34
Pygmalion, 89

Quinn, Kenneth, 96

Rationality versus emotions, Catullan, 11, 13–15
Rejection. *See* Abandonment
Role reversal: in Ovidian poetry, 71; of Propertian lovers, xv, 52, 62, 66
Roman society: adultery as foundation of, 106; brutality toward women in, xv, 89; Catullan defensiveness toward, 21; Catullan rejection of, 14, 19, 27; erotic dominance in, xii; exchange of women among men in, 95, 105; exclusive public and political activity in, 18; family bonds in, 10–11; gender-specific activities in, xii–xiv; imperial values of, 31, 37, 106; *mali* disapproval of passion in, 19, 21–25, 31; masculinity in, xii–xiii, 7; mercantile nature of, 20; moral bankruptcy of, 28, 33; patriarchal values of, xii; rational versus emotional behavior in, 7; self-control in, 7
Rubin, Gayle, 95, 105

Sabine women, 94, 108
Sapphic imagery, 19, 34
Sapphic voice, erotic fragmentation and, 83
Scopophilia, 82
Scylla, 110–11, 119
Segal, Charles, 22
Self-control, 7
Semiramis, in Corinna poem, 78, 80–81, 124
Showalter, Elaine, 19
Sickness, as threat to masculinity, xii
Skinner, Marilyn, 117–18
Sleeping mistress, 55–58, 121
Stahl, Hans-Peter: on apostrophes in Cynthia poems, 46; on war and love imagery, 41, 45
Supernatural, in Ovidian *Amores*, 77–80
Symposium of Plato, 41

Tantalus, 110
Theseus, 56, 86–87
Thesprotus, 61
Time discontinuity, in Catullan poem 8, 3–5, 11
Travel imagery: in Catullan poem 11, 31–32; in Ovidian poem, 96–99
Trojan War, 41

Venus and Mars, 41, 71
Violence: in Cynthia poems, 43; in Ovidian poems, 68
Voices: multiple. *See* Multiple voices *entries*

War and love imagery: Ovidian, 70–71, 73, 95; Propertian, 41
Whore: woman as, 19, 117. *See also* Pimping by Ovidian lover
Witchcraft: Propertian appeal to, 44–45, 120
Woman: chaste, Propertian hatred of, 42; as domesticated product, 95, 105; as field to be ploughed, 25, 76; as goddess or whore, 19, 117; as limit setter, 26; as *materia* (*see* Materia view of woman); materiality and, 25–26; as mistress and mother, 64; as nature, 59; as "other" to Propertian hero, 122; as sexual and economic commodity, xv, 103–4; sleeping, 55–58; as spirited horse, 104; as *tabula rasa*, 58, 63, 89; violence toward, 68; as war booty, 73
Wyke, Maria, 37

LaVergne, TN USA
17 December 2009

167356LV00002B/1/P